ART THIEVES, FAKERS & FRAUDSTERS

art thieves, fakers & fraudsters

the New Zealand story

PENELOPE JACKSON

AWA PRESS

First edition published in 2016 by Awa Press,
Unit 1, Level 3, 11 Vivian Street, Wellington 6011, New Zealand.

ISBN 978-1-927249-51-2

Ebook formats
Epub 978-1-927249-52-9
Mobi 978-1-927249-53-6

A catalogue record for this book is available from the National Library of New Zealand.

Cover image courtesy of
Christchurch Art Gallery Te Puna o Waiwhetu
Author with *A Crown for the Kermadec King* (2010)
by Greg O'Brien: Katie Jones photograph
Cover design by Greg Simpson
Typesetting by Tina Delceg
This book is typeset in Adobe Caslon, William and Founders Grotesk
Printed by 1010 Printing Asia Limited

Produced with the assistance of

creative nz
Arts Council of New Zealand Toi Aotearoa

For my parents, Dorothy and Allan

ALSO BY PENELOPE JACKSON

Edward Bullmore: A Surrealist Odyssey

The Brown Years: Nigel Brown

Corrugations: The Art of Jeff Thomson (co-author)

Terry Stringer – Landscape of the Head

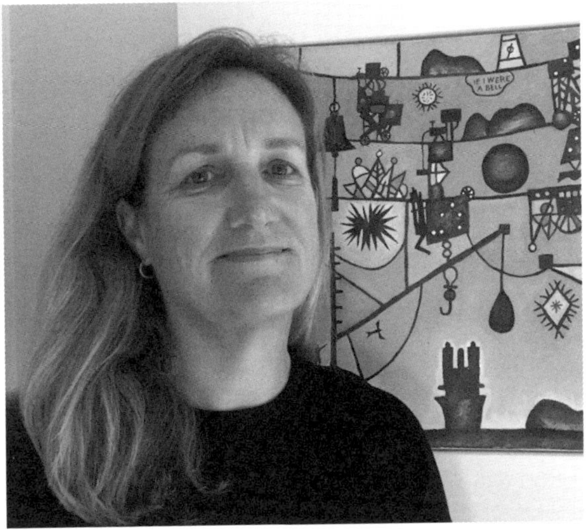

Penelope Jackson is an art historian, an independent curator, a founding member of the New Zealand Art Crime Research Trust, and a former director of Tauranga Art Gallery. She holds degrees in art history from the Universities of Queensland and Auckland, and has contributed to *Art New Zealand*, *Art Monthly Australia*, *Journal of Art Crime* and other publications. She has presented papers at the annual conference in Italy of the international Association for Research into Crimes against Art and the inaugural artcrime2015 symposium at City Gallery, Wellington. Her essay *Legacy and Longevity: Protecting the past for the future* was published in *Art Crime and Its Prevention: A handbook for collectors and art professionals* in 2016.

AUTHOR NOTE

I have endeavoured to fairly represent the artists, dealers, galleries, collectors and others involved in the matters covered in this book, and to seek permission where possible for use of sensitive content. In some cases, parties were invited to read a draft to confirm and/or clarify details. In other cases the person or organisation did not want to engage in dialogue or was deceased. If you have new information, please contact the editorial team at Awa Press. All currency in the book is given in New Zealand dollars unless stated otherwise. All dimensions are in height before width.

Contents

Foreword

I CALL IT THE 'TREASURE HUNT INSTINCT'. We all have it: the desire to find what is lost, to learn what is secret, to see what is hidden, to recover what has vanished. It's no surprise that publishers love to stud their thriller titles with these key words – in fact, it once occurred to me to name one of my books *Lost, Secret, Hidden*. That's the sort of book I would buy without bothering to read what it was about.

This is one of the great appeals of a crime story, whether factual or fictitious. It begins with a question. Something has happened, and we don't know why or how or who did it, or some combination of the above. And something has disappeared, whether an object or a person or a perpetrator. When I teach, I encourage writers to prompt questions in their readers, and then intentionally delay the answer to draw them along. Mysteries and police procedurals do this by their very nature. And when, on our path to answering the questions posed in the crime, we are drawn through an exotic world this is all the more enticing.

The world of art crime intrigues me for just this reason. I was always entranced by art and the opaque, glamorous universe of collectors, galleries, museums, conservators, curators and experts – that wealthy, intelligent, often fraught and sometimes corrupt landscape. This realm is populated by larger than life characters who would be difficult to believe as plausible in a work of fiction. An Irish traveller who is also a bare-knuckle boxing champion helps recover priceless old masters. An oddball loner makes lousy forgeries and passes them off to at least forty galleries, but gives them as gifts, asking nothing in return – and seems not to have broken the law in doing so. An Iranian millionaire art collector, with a lavish collection in his home, is caught slicing rare prints and maps out of books at the British Library. Can any of this be real?

Combine true crime with the pizzazz of the art world, throw in a population of Dickensian caricatures who happen to actually exist, and you have the makings of a sensational book. And this is one such book, swinging the telescope away from the often trod paths of art crime in the United States and Europe (and, lately, the Levant), on to the islands of New Zealand.

There should be a book like this for all 198 nations on the planet: every country has its share of colourful and important stories of crimes involving art. But the truth is that art crime has been largely overlooked until recently, often dismissed as concerning the trifles of the wealthy, an unimportant sort of crime, intriguing and cinematic though it may be.

Fiction and movies are largely to blame. The media tends to focus each year on a half dozen filmic heists from major museums, the ones that make the headlines. Public, police, policymakers and criminals alike 'learn' about art crime at the movies, from Thomas

Crown and Cary Grant and *Ocean's Twelve*. On the one hand, this means that just about anyone you stop on the street will find the subject of interest. On the other hand, it means that no one, not even the authorities, have been taking it too seriously: it feels like a non-threatening, 'victimless' sort of crime, in which you can root for the bad guys because they aren't really all that bad.

It's true that it is extremely rare for violence and art crime to merge. Thank goodness. But it is reductive and uninformed to consider art crime victimless. There are two ways to argue. If you are an art lover, there is of course no need to argue at all. Art, as the zenith of what civilisation is capable, must be protected. If art does not draw out your sympathies, we might point to the criminological argument. Multiple sources, from the United States Department of Justice to UNESCO to Interpol, have labelled art crime as having among the highest-grossing criminal trades worldwide, with tens of thousands of reported art thefts each year – some 20,000 in Italy alone. It is a significant funding source for organised crime groups of all sizes.

Despite this, it is only in the last few years, with the rise of high-profile fundamentalist terrorism in the Levant, that the world has caught up with the experts and realised that art crime is not just interesting but very serious. While the data is not complete, it is clear that illicit looting of antiquities for sale to the West is a major funding source for terrorism. The world has taken notice: beyond the sparkling glamour there lurk shadows.

Thankfully, New Zealand is remote from the rumblings of the Middle East. It is a place where art crime is fascinating, serious and important to curb, but not so scary. It is certainly replete with larger than life characters, but they – at least the forgers among them – tend to be the type with whom you'd like to have a beer. (I can probably do without the gangsters, who can be found in even such an ideal place as New Zealand.)

I first encountered Penelope Jackson's work at the annual conference of ARCA, the Association for Research into Crimes against Art, held every summer in Amelia, Italy, in the midst of ARCA's unique Postgraduate Program in Art Crime and Cultural Heritage Protection, the first interdisciplinary academic programme in the field. Penelope gave a talk on Goldie forgeries, which she writes about in the first chapter of this fine volume. I was immediately impressed. She tells her true crime tales with verve and a keen eye for observation, bringing the characters to life. Most of all, she places them into a criminological and national context, making her stories of interest to New Zealanders by holding up a mirror to their own darker sides and the penumbral recesses of their cultural history. And for foreign readers the locale of New Zealand adds intrigue and colour, for while most writers on art crime deal in the same few dozen retold tales of high-profile European events (I'm guilty as charged), the lesser-known stories are often the freshest and offer the most enlightenment.

Let's take a walk, then, along new trails, blazed in a place that is beautiful and, for most of us, far-flung, guided by a true expert.

Dr Noah Charney
Founder, Association for Research into Crimes against Art

Introduction

LIKE MANY ART HISTORIANS it was my dream to rediscover a forgotten artist and tell his or her story. My chance came in 2003 when I was mesmerised by a painting hanging in Tauranga City Library. *Derelict* was by Edward Bullmore, who had painted it in 1957 at the age of twenty-four. It depicted an abandoned wooden boat washed up on the mudflats of Tauranga Harbour, and seemed to me to have been influenced by two doyens of the Canterbury school of landscape painting, Russell Clark and Bill Sutton. However, the painting had a surrealist aspect that was at odds with the school's teachings. Bullmore was clearly pushing the boundaries. *Derelict* was enchanting – beautiful, well painted, and on display in, of all places, a city that was bereft of a public art gallery and showed little interest in preserving its artistic and cultural heritage.

Eager to find out everything I could about Bullmore, I quickly discovered there was little written about him, and yet he had had a burgeoning international career in the 1960s. He had indeed studied at the Canterbury School of Fine Arts. His paintings had featured in the cult movie *A Clockwork Orange*, and hung alongside works by Jean Miro, Giorgio de Chirico, Max Ernst, Salvador Dalí, Yves Tanguy, Paul Klee, André Masson, René Magritte, André Breton and Pablo Picasso in an exhibition, *The Enchanted Domain: Surrealist Art* in Exeter, England in 1967. His achievements had, meanwhile, gone almost unnoticed in his homeland.

As I dug deeper over the following months I learned to my surprise that behind Bullmore's exciting body of work lay a story of intrigue. More than 150 of his works had simply disappeared while being supposedly minded by his younger brother. As I researched and wrote up Bullmore's life and work for a retrospective exhibition, the complexity of locating his works, and troubling questions around their ownership, whetted my appetite. Had the works been stolen? And if so was this an isolated case? Or was art crime taking place on an extensive scale in New Zealand?

AMERICAN CRIMINOLOGIST JOHN CONKLIN has defined art crimes as criminally punishable acts that involve works of art.[1] The definition is justifiably broad. Such crimes include straight-out theft, fraud in the form of forgeries and fakes, vandalism, wartime confiscations, and association with other crimes, such as artefacts being used as bargaining chips.

For most people, knowledge about art crime comes from sensationalist media reports of high-profile cases, such as the revelation in 2016 that the august Alexander Turnbull Library, a department of the New Zealand National Library charged with collecting heritage material, had purchased a fake Lindauer despite being told it was probably just that, and from movies with handsome male leads, such as *The Thomas Crown Affair*, *Gambit* and *The Monuments Men*. In reality art crime is far from glamorous. In my search for information I have not come across any villains or victims remotely resembling Pierce Brosnan, Colin Firth or George Clooney.

Although many of the books and movies are the products of vivid imagining, this is a realm where truth can be stranger than fiction. Real events, such as the discovery in 2012 of a major collection of more than 1,200 artworks looted by the Nazis and sequestered in a Munich apartment for six decades, have captivated the world. The owner of the apartment, Cornelius Gurlitt, was the son of an art historian and picture dealer who had been under orders from Hitler's minister of propaganda, Joseph Goebbels, to amass modern artworks for a vast museum Hitler planned to build in Linz, his hometown in Austria.[2] The case helped stimulate greater awareness of historical art crimes, and offered fresh hope that stolen artworks could still be recovered more than half a century later.

THE QUESTION I ASKED MYSELF was how New Zealand fitted into this picture. Did this country too have a history of art thefts, fakes and forgeries? I quickly found it was not an easy question to answer. Many cases go unreported. Those that are reported rarely receive specialist attention from the police. In this we follow much of the rest of the world. Art crime specialist Noah Charney observed in *The Art Newspaper* in December 2013 that police forces seldom distinguish between stolen art and other stolen goods. 'A Rembrandt,' Charney noted, 'is classified with a CD.'

In New Zealand little attention has been given to classifying art crime, and the police force is too small to support the sort of art crime squads or art loss agencies that exist in other countries.

In late 2015 Dr Catherine Gardner of the New Zealand Police, preparing to address the inaugural symposium of the New Zealand Art Crime Research Trust, researched 'theft of art' in police records. Ninety-three cases had been registered since recording began. Most were not well defined and the file often appeared to be a dumping ground for difficult and obscure cases. One record concerned the theft of a person's hair extensions.

When I began researching art crime in New Zealand, the task felt at once daunting and exciting. Initial searches threw up a large amount of material, mainly newspaper clippings. I began to get a sense of the scale and enormity of the work ahead. In August 2013 Kathryn Ryan interviewed me on her Radio New Zealand programme *Nine to Noon*. Within minutes of the interview ending a number of people had contacted me with their own stories. Some wanted to know if I could help them locate missing artworks. Others asked if there was a book on the subject. There seemed to be a big story to tell.

One thing, though, surprised me. I was no stranger to research: I had curated exhibitions and worked in public art galleries for most of my career and found organisations and individuals usually helpful and generous in adding to our canon of art history. Yet when it came to art crime a number of people actively avoided my quest for information. I was sometimes challenged as to whether shining a light on these activities and opening old wounds was helpful to the art world. Some institutions wanted to conceal the fact that artworks had been stolen from them, or they had purchased or otherwise acquired paintings of dubious provenance. I came across roadblocks where information was kept strictly confidential and thus unobtainable.

Perhaps I should not have been surprised. Art crime, especially theft, had been on my radar for a while – and in one case had come very close to home. In 2011 nine New Zealand artists had been invited by an American environmental group, the Pew Charitable Trusts, to sail to the Kermadec Islands, which lie in a largely pristine area of New Zealand territorial waters. Out of this voyage had come a touring exhibition originating at the Tauranga Art Gallery Toi Tauranga, where I was director. Two days before Christmas two small canvases, each 100 x 100 mm, went missing from the exhibition. The work of artist John Reynolds, the canvases were part of an installation of 113 works, all the same size, called *Wakey, Wakey, Wakey*. Displayed to Reynolds' specifications in a random-looking pile, the works were counted every morning and evening by gallery staff, but because of their small size it had proved easy enough for someone to slip two of them into a bag.

Fortunately the artist was happy to supply replacement works but for gallery staff the theft was a wake-up call. It had happened right under our noses, despite security cameras and diligent observation. Not wanting the public to realise the small canvases were an easy target, I had not reported the incident to the police or media. This is not unusual: victims of art crime may not go public for fear of inspiring and encouraging copycat crimes. And for art galleries there is another consideration: as organisations reliant on the goodwill of private lenders and other galleries and museums, we do not want to raise any doubts around the security of our premises.

This book includes some cases that have received a lot of public attention and others that have been kept quiet for a variety of reasons. It is the first comprehensive report on art crime in New Zealand but I am sure it will not be the last. Just as technological and scientific advances are making it easier for such crimes to be committed, they are also making it easier for them to be detected. Behind traditional art history, then, there increasingly lies this alternative history, at once fascinating and shocking.

ONE

Gold from Goldies

IN 2008 A RETIRED COUPLE, Bill and Phyllis Gibson, decided to sell their house in Mosgiel, south of Dunedin. Sometime between July and October that year a portrait by C.F. Goldie that had been hanging in their house disappeared. At first the Gibsons didn't notice the painting was missing. It had been on a wall behind a door in a spare bedroom and the thief had cleverly hung another painting in its place.

The missing portrait was of a Māori woman with a moko, a traditional facial tattoo; she was looking back over her shoulder, and her hair was tied back. The painting had been in the Gibson family for more than six decades, having been given to Phyllis Gibson's parents by the artist as a token of thanks for their care and teaching of Māori in south Taranaki: her father had been a teacher in the Waitotara area and her mother a nurse.

According to the couple, the only inscription on the back was a note about the gifting. It read something like: 'In appreciation of B. Whiteside's work with Māori in Waitotara Area. C.F. Goldie.'

As is often the case with domestic art collections, neither the title nor the date of the painting was recorded. In fact there was no actual evidence of the painting's existence. Since it had been a gift there was no record of purchase, and as it had stayed in the same family the entire time there was no paper trail of provenance. And the work had never been photographed.

The timing of the painting's disappearance led the owners to conclude it had probably been stolen during an open home when their house was on the market and visited by potential buyers and interested onlookers. Unfortunately, the real estate agent who had organised the open homes had moved on, and the agency had not retained the list of visitors that would have been collected at the time.

Once the media were alerted to the story, a television channel hastened to interview Bill Gibson. The case had all the ingredients of a good story – a Goldie painting, a brazen theft, a real estate open home and an elderly couple. In hindsight, it is likely the attention was detrimental to the chances of solving the crime: publicity like this can dissuade a thief or handler of stolen property from trying to sell the goods, making it more difficult for the police to track them down and apprehend those responsible. The Gibsons had provided a good description of the painting, and they hoped that if it had been offered for sale to a dealer gallery or through an auction, the police would learn of it. In the event, the painting has never been seen again and its fate is unknown.

WHEN NEWS OF THE THEFT reached the public, Roger Blackley, an art historian and eminent Goldie scholar, noted that the artist's paintings regularly went on holiday, a polite way of saying they are regular targets for thieves. Charles Frederick Goldie, born in Auckland in 1870, is often considered New Zealand's greatest nineteenth-century artist. As a young man he travelled to Paris and studied art at the Académie Julian. On his return he began painting finely detailed portraits of Māori kuia and chiefs. These portraits were enormously popular and remain so today. Goldie was a master salesman, even producing carefully crafted studio photographs that romantically depicted the artist at work with his sitters.

Goldie has been referred to as New Zealand's Rembrandt – an apt comparison since deception also figures largely in that painter's story. Those who have tried to establish a complete catalogue of Rembrandt's work have found that the number of authentic paintings is somewhere between 250 and 350, half the number previously thought. The discrepancy is explained by the number of assistants Rembrandt had working for him and painting in his style. His pupils also emulated his style.

Similarly, Goldie's oeuvre has been difficult to catalogue with absolute certainty. In his 1997 book on the artist, Blackley warned there was no comfort to be had from information adhered to the reverse side of Goldie paintings. 'It should be noted,' he wrote, 'that several of the forged Goldie paintings that have appeared in recent years [have] come complete with such a label, itself a forgery of Goldie's distinctive script.'

Goldie was one of the few artists of his generation to make a comfortable living from his art. His studio in central Auckland was conveniently located for his patrons, and for his customers, who included tourists visiting the city by ship. He regularly took as subjects Māori who were attending hearings at the nearby Native Land Court and were introduced to him by Robert McVeagh, a solicitor fluent in Māori who often attended hearings at the court.

Commercially astute, Goldie paid his sitters a meagre fee and regularly copied his own works.

As Goldie's career developed he took up opportunities to exhibit overseas. In the early 1930s three of his paintings were shown at the Royal Academy in London, and he exhibited regularly with the Salon de Paris throughout the decade. This made his work even more desirable and Goldie did not shy away from pricing it at the high end of the market. At the 1904 Canterbury Society of Arts annual exhibition both portraits he put up for sale had price tags of more than £27 while oil paintings by other artists were priced at less than £10. One of Goldie's contemporaries, Sydney Lough Thompson, who also painted Māori portraits and had trained in France, was much less financially successful. In 1910, when both men exhibited at the Canterbury Society of Arts, Goldie's *Tikitere Mihi*, a portrait of an Arawa chief, was priced at £73.10.0 and Thompson's *Aged Warrior* at only £50.

Goldie's painting technique required little deconstruction by the viewer. His portraits, which carried titles such as *Forty Winks*, *Planning Revenge*, *A Hot Day* and *A Noble Relic of a Noble Race*, were formulaic in both composition and choice of palette. Their heavy black frames, made of native timbers, harked back to Rembrandt and the Dutch golden age and were designed to project an 'old master' image. Because the paintings are such prototypes, when one goes missing its owners can usually supply very little information that will identify it: their descriptions could apply to many Goldie portraits. However, as Ngahiraka Mason, the former curator of Māori art at Auckland Art Gallery Toi o Tāmaki, has suggested, Goldie's portraits provide an irreplacable record of ancestors.

Today many collectors assume a Goldie painting is a safe investment, as buyers did a century ago. The works are easily recognisable and resale is almost guaranteed. They regularly hit the headlines for the prices fetched at auction, and these are often the highest in a sale. In 1984 Peter Webb, an art auctioneer, predicted that any Goldie portrait had the potential to sell for more than $100,000. Four years later one sold for $110,000. In 1976 it had sold for $18,000.

In 1991 the National Art Gallery – now the Museum of New Zealand Te Papa Tongarewa – helped push up the value of Goldie paintings when it paid an astonishing one million dollars for a pair of 1903 portraits, *Ina Te Papatahi, A Ngapuhi Chieftainess* and *The Widow (Harata Rewiri Tarapata, Ngapuhi)*, known colloquially as Darby and Joan.

Goldie paintings continued to appreciate. In 2008 Auckland's International Art Centre reported that its top five sales were Goldie portraits. Prices ranged from $165,000 to $400,000. In the same year another auction house, Dunbar Sloane in Wellington, sold *A Noble Relic of a Noble Race*, believed to be Goldie's last painting, for over $400,000. Even at a time of economic recession, the sale reached the top end of the estimated reserve. The subject, Wharekauri Tahuna, a Ngāti Manawa and Tūhoe priest and chief, was believed to be 102 years old when he sat for Goldie, and is the subject of three other Goldie portraits, two of which are in Auckland War Memorial Museum and Te Papa respectively. In March 2016, the painting sold for $1.3 million, the highest price ever paid at auction for a New Zealand painting.

In 2010 the internationally renowned opera singer Dame Kiri Te Kanawa put *Forty Winks*, a Goldie portrait of Rutene Te Uamairangi from her personal collection, up for sale. In its announcement of the coming auction, the International Art Centre mentioned the work's remarkable provenance: it had been owned not only by Dame Kiri but also, until 1948, by Goldie's wife, Olive. As Dame Kiri had been just four years old in 1948, the painting must have had at least one other owner but this was not mentioned. Perhaps the name of the other owner, or owners, had not been recorded. This lack of a complete provenance did not deter buyers. The sale attracted considerable media hype and the painting fetched $573,000.

FOR AN INVESTOR with little specialist art knowledge, a Goldie painting is seen as a dead cert. When in 2009 the Auckland Art Gallery announced that American millionaires Julian and Josie Robertson had gifted it a valuable art collection that included works by Picasso, Cézanne, Gauguin and Mondrian, the prime minister, John Key, was quick to point out that Goldie was his favourite artist. He would, he said, rather have a Goldie than a Picasso or a Cézanne.[3]

Many purchase a Goldie work with the intention of on-selling it and making a tidy sum. A Tauranga grocer told me he had purchased a Goldie portrait in lieu of a pension fund. He might be lucky – or not. Like many investors, he could have unknowingly purchased a forgery or stolen work.

In the six decades since Goldie's death, criminal activity has swirled around the artist's work. The catalogue of thefts demonstrates the lengths to which perpetrators will go. On September 7, 1973 two works – *Memories, Te Hei, A chieftainess of the Ngatiraukawe* (1909) and *Pipi puzzled* (1919) – were stolen from the National Art Gallery in Wellington. Both portraits were hurriedly removed from their frames and the thieves made a rapid exit. At the time each work was valued at $6,000. They were subsequently located after a Taupō police detective, Rex Hawkins, received information that they were being offered for sale in the area.

George Packwood, the curator of the National Art Gallery, wrote about what happened when he helped police retrieve the paintings by posing as a well-known art historian, Gordon Brown.

> Arrived at Rotorua 12 midday and was taken in rental car to Wairakei. At Huka Falls, met the rest of police and plans were outlined. From there proceeded to Wairakei Golf Club, where we stayed until 3.45 p.m., and then on to Wairakei Hotel, where a room was booked for me to pose as expert on Goldie paintings. After a short time a man was brought to the room carrying a pillowslip from which two packages were taken. One of these contained the two Goldies, which were given to me to inspect. The man who brought the pictures in informed me he knew they were genuine because they came from the Auckland Museum. … I said I could not guarantee the Goldies as the real thing. The buyer said he would not take them under these circumstances. … As soon as he had gone the police were informed … and the man was arrested.

The Goldie works had sustained minor damage when they were cut from their frames. On December 1, Phillip Wayne Allen was charged with stealing the two paintings. The informant was paid $1,200, a considerable sum at the time.

Public reaction to the crime was mixed. Many people were appalled that paintings had been stolen so easily from a national institution, but someone distributed a flyer that proclaimed: 'They've gone missing! Isn't it marvellous!' Possibly the person simply didn't like Goldie's work, but he or she may just as well have viewed the artist as a ruthless entrepreneur who made a good living out of painting Māori sitters while paying them poorly. Feelings towards Goldie's work have always been mixed.

THE SAME YEAR the National Art Gallery's Goldie paintings went missing, another opportunist set to work at Auckland Grammar School, a prestigious boys' secondary school that had been founded in 1868 and attended by Goldie himself. A Goldie painting *The Dignity of the Maori Ngaheke*, also known as *Perira Te Kahi*, had been gifted to the school in 1948 by Eliot Davis, a former student, prominent businessman, member of the Legislative Council, and racehorse owner. The painting hung in the school hall. In 1973, perhaps as a result of media coverage of the National Art Gallery heist, it was stolen, although it was later returned.

On February 9, 1987 the school's art collection was again targeted and, as well as an early lithographic print of a Māori chief from a Goldie portrait, three other valuable works were stolen: *Portrait of Sir George Grey* by Louis John Steele (an oil painting measuring 500 x 450 mm); *A View of a West Coast Gorge* by John Barr Clark Hoyte (a watercolour, 600 x 350 mm); and *Eleven Forty-Three and Still No Sign of the Train* by George Baloghy (acrylic on canvas, 920 x 615 mm) dated 1981.The total estimated value of the works was around $55,000. All had been removed from their frames.

The Baloghy painting was found soon afterwards in a gutter on the corner of Shore Road and Burwood Crescent in the suburb of Remuera. It had been folded eight times so it resembled a small package. Neither the Hoyte nor Steele work has ever been found.

The Dignity of the Maori Ngaheke was not taken this time, but it is not unusual for a work to be stolen repeatedly. Jan van Eyck's multi-panel masterpiece *Ghent Altarpiece*, completed in 1432, has been stolen from its home in Ghent's Saint Bavo Cathedral seven times, including by German forces in the First and Second World Wars. It has also been burned, forged, illegally sold, and attacked by iconoclasts. One panel is still at large.

In 1981 a Goldie painting, *The Scribe*, was stolen from the Dowse Art Museum in Lower Hutt. The theft, which was reported in *The Evening Post*, exposed problems with the Dowse's security system: the perpetrator had taken the painting from an unlocked temporary storage space in an area with supposedly restricted access. The gallery was unsure when this had happened and admitted the painting may have been missing for as long as two months. Local auction house Dunbar Sloane had valued *The Scribe* at $15,000 to $20,000. According to the Dowse it was the first piece of art to go missing from the ten-year-old gallery.

Three days later a rendezvous was orchestrated between police and a third party. *The Evening Post* noted that 'the party who returned the painting would not be the basis of the police enquiry'. No one was ever charged with the theft.

Embarrassingly for the gallery, it did not own the stolen painting but was caretaking it for a private collector. How well a work is secured and protected from damage, vandalism and theft can be integral to attracting gifts and loans for public collections. To protect a work fully a museum or gallery may need to place stanchions and safety glass around it and alarm it individually, as well as have security staff patrolling the exhibition space. This can be achieved in large institutions, but smaller regional galleries are typically constrained by their budgets.

And there's another problem: barricades around an artwork can diminish the experience for viewers, and uniformed security guards make an exhibition space seem uninviting. Such issues are international. London's Dulwich Picture Gallery has had a small 1632 Rembrandt portrait of Jacob de Gheyn III stolen four times – in 1966, 1973, 1981 and 1983 – because it cannot provide the level of security required. Known as the 'Takeaway Rembrandt', the painting is so well known to the public that any thief would have great difficulty selling it and any purchaser would have to be extraordinarily careful when exhibiting it. However, this does not seem to lessen its appeal as a target.

The *Mona Lisa*, arguably the world's most famous painting, was stolen by a misguided Italian patriot in 1911 (he was caught two years later and the painting returned), and has been attacked several times, including being sprayed with red paint in 1974 and having a cup hurled at it in 2009. The bulletproof glass installed to protect it has kept Leonardo da Vinci's masterpiece undamaged.

THE RATE OF RECOVERY of stolen Goldie paintings is small and this is consistent with art theft worldwide. In December 2013 *The Art Newspaper* reported that internationally as little as 1.5 percent of all stolen art is recovered, although the rate is higher for famous works because of the difficulty of reselling them. As artworks are original and ireplaceable, there can be more value placed on their safe return than on punishing the criminals. Deals behind the scenes are common. While some thieves steal a work for their personal pleasure, others plan to use it to bargain their way out of another crime, or to make a political gesture.

It's not only theft that has plagued the works of Charles Frederick Goldie. Many of his paintings have been vandalised. Early one afternoon in November 1944 a portrait, *Ena Papatai* (today known as *Portrait of Ina te Papatahi, A Ngapuhi Chieftainess)*, along with five other paintings in Christchurch's Robert McDougall Art Gallery, was scratched with a knife. The incident took only fifteen minutes. The vandal was never caught. The journal *Art in New Zealand* noted that the gallery was perhaps too secluded on its Botanic Gardens site: another important work, Solomon J. Solomon's *Psyche*, had been stolen just two years earlier.

Vandalising art is a crime under New Zealand's Summary Offences Act 1981. Although the damaged goods instantly lose market value, the punishment for perpetrators is surprisingly mild: 'A person is liable to a community-based sentence or a fine not exceeding $2,000, or to both, if he or she damages or defaces any building, structure, road, tree, property, or other thing by writing, drawing, painting, spraying, or etching on it, or otherwise marking it.'

Art vandalism is usually premeditated, and often carried out despite the presence of gallery and museum staff. Motives range from making a political statement to simply seeking attention. Scissors, spray paint, keys, acid and knives are just some of the tools used. But damage can also occur as a side effect of a poorly planned and executed theft. Larger works suffer the most as they are more difficult to move quickly from a crime scene, and are often ripped from their stretchers and frames.[4]

IN SEPTEMBER 1998 a suspicious-looking man wearing a long coat entered the Dunedin Public Art Gallery in the city's Octagon. He immediately walked up to a 1941 Goldie painting, *Rahapa, Ohinemutu*, which was on loan from a private collection, and spray-painted a red peace sign on it. Gallery staff acted quickly both to apprehend the man and remove the paint. The conservator, Titus

Chan, spent forty minutes lightly wiping the painting's surface in a circular motion with a mild turpentine-based solvent and cotton swabs held with tweezers.

'My hand was shaking,' he told the *Otago Daily Times*. 'It's a very valuable artwork. It was worth thousands and thousands of dollars, so it was important not to damage the surface.'

The vandal, a 44-year-old sickness beneficiary, pleaded guilty and was fined $750, plus court costs of $130 and reparation of $295. Fortunately, the painting was able to be returned to its original state.

The crimes associated with Goldie's work may seem small in scale compared to international art crimes, but within the context of New Zealand's art history they are significant since the Goldie portraits are so valuable and sought-after. But why are these works targeted? Is it possible that some of the vandalism and theft is in revenge for cultural insensitivities of the past? Do Māori feel that their ancestors were exploited by the artist for monetary gain? Do they believe these portraits of ancestors should be returned to their iwi?

Such questions have continued in the art world as well as in the wider community. As Roger Blackley noted in a short biography of Goldie, while some descendants of Goldie's models have hailed the depictions of their ancestors, others have denounced them as racist. An Auckland Art Gallery media release announcing a Goldie exhibition that toured in 1998–9 noted that while Goldie's work was 'surrounded by controversy like the work of no other New Zealand artist', the hauntingly lifelike paintings remained compelling.

'Whether he is "our greatest painter",' the release went on, 'an "outdated, academic racist" or no more than a "second-rate Lindauer", one thing is certain: the debate surrounding the work of our most well-known painter shows no sign of fading quietly away.'

IN JANUARY 2007, during the Christmas–New Year break, a thief forced a window of the University of Auckland library and made off with a Goldie portrait, as well as an Oxford Lectern Bible from the 1930s, and a framed set of seven manuscript poems by New Zealand's leading twentieth-century modernist artist, Colin McCahon. This was classic timing: as was the case with the theft of two of John Reynolds' *Wakey, Wakey, Wakey* canvases, thieves often strike during a holiday period. In 2009 a heist of thirty works, including a Picasso and a Matisse, from Fasanengalerie, a private gallery near west Berlin's central shopping district, also took place during the New Year period.

Another famous case, which remains unsolved, was a St Patrick's Day heist of thirteen works from Boston's Isabella Stewart Gardner Museum. Included in the haul were works by Rembrandt and Vermeer. While the city was preoccupied with commemorating the death of Ireland's patron saint, thieves spent eighty-one minutes in the museum, making their selection and dealing with the two security guards, art students who had been trained only the week before. The unfortunate students were handcuffed to pipes, and duct tape was placed around their hands, feet and heads.

Planning Revenge: Portrait of Hori Pokai, the Goldie work stolen from the library, had been gifted to the university by its Canadian owners, Diana and Gordon Green. Diana Green had inherited the portrait from her mother, who had purchased it while visiting Auckland in the 1930s. It had been on display in the library for less than a month. Helene Philips, a local gallery owner, noted that if the Goldie portrait and the other works had been stolen to order they would probably disappear into a collection and never be seen again.

However ten months later, in October 2007, *The New Zealand Herald* reported that a deal had been struck between police and a criminal known only as 'W'. Although not the thief, W was using his information about the location of the missing works to plea-bargain himself out of unrelated charges that were about to be heard in the Auckland District Court, a situation a local newspaper labelled 'unorthodox'. All the stolen works were returned.

In 2008 *Sunday News* reported a conversation with W's father about the day his son had brought home the stolen portrait.

'He asked me, "Do you want to see a nice painting?"

'I said, "That's a Goldie. It's beautiful. Where did you get that from?"

'He said, "No questions."'

Fortunately, the principal conservator of the Auckland Art Gallery, Sarah Hillary, had just completed a conservation report on the painting; it was inspected and ascertained not to have sustained any damage. When it was returned, security was increased throughout the library and a long-term security review carried out to try and prevent further thefts.

But a question remains: why had the thief chosen to steal the Goldie portrait rather than any other work in the university's 800-strong collection? Works in the collection were, and still are, on permanent display across four campuses in Auckland city, as well as in temporary exhibitions at the university's Gus Fisher Gallery. Perhaps the thieves, inspired by the painting's name, were literally out for revenge?

TWO

The forger

GIVEN GOLDIE'S POPULARITY and the strong demand for his work, one forger found a niche market. His success has meant that trying to ascertain if a 'Goldie' is the genuine item has added greatly to the intrigue surrounding the artist's paintings.

First a note about terminology. The terms 'fake' and 'forgery' are often used interchangeably but in fact they have different meanings. A fake work of art is one that is created to resemble, but not duplicate, existing ones by an artist. This is sometimes called 'in the style of'. A forgery is a work made with the intention of passing it off as the original. Usually the intention is to sell it as such. Both practices are tantamount to fraud.

The fraudsters' methods can be very sophisticated. As John Conklin wrote in his 1994 book *Art Crime*:

> They go to extraordinary lengths to copy the materials used by the artists whose works they are counterfeiting, mixing paints from the same ingredients, using old canvas to paint on, and artificially aging their fakes

> and forgeries by cracking the surface varnish of oil paintings and 'stressing' statues and pottery.

And as Noah Charney has noted, if a forger is charged it is usually with the crime of fraud: there is no crime of forgery per se.

ENTER KARL SIM. Born in the small settlement of Mangaweka in 1923, Sim attended Palmerston North Technical College, where he was taught by the well-known and respected artist Harry Linley Richardson. Richardson had painted several portraits of Māori and this, along with Sim's love of C.F. Goldie's portraiture, may have sparked Sim's interest in Māori as subjects for art. As a teenager he had attended an exhibition of Richardson's and Goldie's work at the local art society with his parents, met Goldie and been awestruck.

When he left school he didn't undertake formal art training, instead working on the family farm at Himatangi, north of Wellington. He then did a short stint in the army. In the 1950s he opened a store in the small town of Foxton on the busy main road north from Wellington, where he sold a variety of goods, including cheap port wine, art and second-hand goods. He sometimes held auctions, dabbled in real estate, and gained a reputation as a local character.

From the late 1960s Sim began to copy paintings, selling the copies as originals. As the business grew he couldn't believe his luck. He would later reflect, 'I didn't come to forgery, it came to me.' In 1977 he was excited to sell a forged Goldie for $2,500. Over the next thirty years he copied the work of Goldie and at least sixty other dead artists, including Rita Angus and the Dutch-born landscape painter Petrus van der Velden, who had settled in Christchurch in 1890 and made a big impression with his sublime and energetic images of Ōtira Gorge on the West Coast.

With each work, Sim would provide a false provenance. In *Good as Goldie*, a book he later co-wrote with journalist Tim Wilson, he confessed: 'I'd chuck in props like fabricated letters and phoney receipts. I often used a recently deceased widow; one of those always helped a provenance no end.'

He made little attempt to hide his activities. His business card – which offered all kinds of services, among them 'tiger taming' – advertised 'Painting by any World Artist to order'. He took particular pleasure in deceiving buyers for large private and public collections.

Arrested in 1985 on forty-eight charges, including twenty-five of forgery and twenty of 'uttering' – issuing forged documents to support forged artworks – and three other kinds of fraud, he changed his name by deed poll to 'Carl Feodor Goldie', thereby assuming the surname and initials of the famous artist.

During Sim's trial the following year, much attention was paid to a collection of thirty-six Petrus van der Velden pencil-and-crayon sketches, many two-sided, that had been purchased by the National Art Gallery five years earlier. Sim recalled: 'I loved watching the experts handling my "van der Velden" sketches wearing white gloves, so they didn't damage this valuable artwork.'

As is the case with any acquisition made by a public organisation, the National Art Gallery had prepared an acquisition report for the van der Velden sketches, stating why they would benefit the gallery's collection and giving background information. Anne Kirker, the curator, had gone to the trouble of having the sketches checked by Rodney Wilson, who was an expert on the artist's work and author of a 1977 book about him. Wilson confirmed the works were authentic. In the report it was noted that Wilson 'confirmed style, subject matter + signature as early v.d.Velden, 1867–69'. Three other gallery staff had also examined the sketches and decided they were by Petrus van der Velden. The purchase went ahead. Sim was paid $5,500.

It would later emerge that Wilson had confirmed the works' authenticity without actually sighting them. Instead he had worked from photocopies and correspondence held by the National Art Gallery in which Sim had provided 'provenance' for the sketches. In a letter on his business letterhead dated December 5, 1979, Sim explained that he had visited a very close friend at Wellington Hospital, a Mrs Grace Martin. Martin had presented him with a folder of drawings and stated that she wished him to have them as a gift from her family. They were of some value and he could do what he liked with them. He was also gifted other art works and taonga Māori. Mrs Martin had apparently organised all this just a few days before she died, with her son Roderick, who lived in Australia, in attendance.

During Sim's trial, John West, a forensic document examiner and witness for the prosecution, noted that all signatures on the drawings shared characteristics with Sim's handwriting. There were also inconsistencies in grammar and spelling. Some signatures had a capital 'V' in 'van' and Velden was sometimes spelled 'Veldon'. (It is also worth noting that artists don't usually sign every individual sketch, especially those made in a sketchbook.) Despite such errors, Sim's work had been convincing enough for the National Art Gallery to acquire the collection, and the works had been catalogued as van der Veldens.

The case raised an interesting question: what should an institution do with works they own that are found to be fakes or forgeries? De-accessioning works is complex and a national museum cannot ethically release forgeries back on to the open market. The National Art Gallery chose to keep the bogus van der Veldens but they have never been exhibited: the use of public funds to purchase forgeries is not something an illustrious national gallery would want to advertise. Recently the sketches have been recatalogued as works by Karl Sim.

TWO TYPES OF ANALYSES are carried out in an attempt to establish whether a work is authentic. The first is a stylistic analysis by a professional such as an art historian. He or she looks at the signature for inconsistencies. They consider where and how the work might fit into the artist's oeuvre, including physical characteristics such as the work's size, and its frame if there is one. They study the paint and other material that make up the work. A person with specialist knowledge about a particular artist will recognise deviations in the way the paint or other substances have been applied and in the colour palette used. They will also look at how information has been recorded on the back of the work and whether this conforms to the artist's usual practice.

The second type of analysis, known as technical, is usually carried out by a conservator. It involves literally looking into the work. The ability to X-ray an artwork was a breakthrough in the 1890s. For the first time it was possible to see what was beneath the painted surface without physically harming the work. The technique's first major use was in a trial in the United States in the 1920, when it was used in an attempt – unsuccessfully as it turned out – to establish whether a certain painting was by Leonardo da Vinci.

More recently carbon dating, invented in the late 1940s, has been used. A biopsy is taken from the work and the paint or other substance used is analysed. Although this is a more intrusive method, and accurate to only plus or minus forty years, it can be definitive in proving whether the substance used to create the work is of a type used by the artist and appropriate for the era. The visible surface of a painting is also integral to determining its age. The craquelure – the network of fine cracks in the paint or varnish – can show what lies underneath. The pattern of cracking can also be compared with that of other works by the same artist.

Both types of analyses help determine authenticity. As Marjorie Wieseman, curator of Dutch and Flemish painting at the National Gallery in London, pointed out in her 2010 book *A Closer Look*: 'objective scientific examination can ... balance historical assessments driven by a desire to recognise great works by iconic artists.'

AMONG THE TECHNIQUES Sim used to make paintings and sketches look genuine was imbedding pieces of newspaper into the plaster of the backing board, as though Goldie had done it. He stockpiled old newspapers, which he may have acquired during his business activities: on his stationery he called himself a licensed antique dealer. In one instance cited in court he had carefully removed a piece of newspaper dated November 21, 1918 and stuck it on to the back of a sketch signed 'C F Goldie'. Unfortunately for Sim, when the police searched his property in August 1984 they found the newspaper, minus the piece stuck to the sketch. Another piece of evidence against Sim was his occasional use of Grumbacher art paper: this had been available in New Zealand only since 1956, a decade after Goldie's death.

Sim's court hearing took seven weeks – once it got started. He managed to delay it by deliberately jumping through a damaged ceiling at his shop to injure himself. His first attempt failed but on the second he broke several ribs and was bedridden for a few months. When the trial finally got underway it was a media sensation and many people, especially the owners of Goldie paintings, watched it with interest, fearing their precious works might be forgeries. Convicted on most charges, Sim was fined $1,000 and sentenced to 200 hours' community service. He was proud he had avoided a prison sentence. The maximum penalty for his offences was ten years in jail and his lawyer, Ken Bailey, had told him he might receive at least seven years. His community service involved painting the Foxton Council Chambers and four public toilet blocks. In typical fashion Sim left his mark, signing C F Goldie in several places.

In 1987 he unsuccessfully appealed his convictions. The Court of Appeal concluded all convictions had to stand. 'Not surprisingly,' the court noted, 'there has been no appeal against what appears to have been a lenient sentence of 200 hours' community work and a fine of $1,000.'

CRIMINAL CONVICTIONS DIDN'T STOP Sim continuing to deal and dabble in art, although from then on he sold his works as 'forgeries' not 'originals'. Thomas Hoving, the former director of the Metropolitan Museum of Art in New York and a noted fake-buster, observed in 1997 that the art crime 'profession' was 'populated by miscreants who say they fake only to show up how stupid, blind, and pompous the art establishment is'. This was true of Karl Sim. Shortly after his death in 2013 aged nearly ninety, his sister, Margaret Jones, told a reporter for *The New Zealand Herald*: 'He didn't do it for money or anything. He did it to beat the establishment, because arty people can get a bit snooty. Beating them was his main aim.' Sim was not, however, immune to the charms of money. In 2008 he had admitted:

> I hoped to receive about $20,000 for the lot but the dealer offered me $6,000. Even so, I couldn't get down there quick enough to collect the money. Beating experts is the loveliest thing in the world.

There may well have been another motivation. Forgers are sometimes frustrated artists. Certainly, as a young man, Sim had harboured an ambition to be a working artist. He put in the hours but never sold anything. As he wryly observed in his 2003 autobiography, who was going to buy a painting by an unknown called K Sim? What he could do, and with considerable skill, was copy the work of eminent artists.

A few years ago, after my interview on Radio New Zealand, I received a letter from another of Sim's sisters, Peach Eaton. She chastised me for not understanding Sim's work. Her brother, she said, had never made any money from his art but dealers had certainly profited from 'his Goldies'. She went on to suggest that I needed to study more, implying that what Sim had done was perfectly acceptable. Eaton was clearly proud of her brother's ability as a copyist.

INTERESTINGLY, COPYING FAMOUS WORKS OF ART is a common practice in art schools, and sometimes these legitimate copies, done to study and perfect artistic techniques, can make their way out into the art market. My initiation to this came when, early in my career, I worked at the Robert McDougall Art Gallery in Christchurch. Each fortnight I profiled an item from the gallery's collection and my articles were published in *The Press*. In one of these articles I profiled *Welcome Morsels* by Leonard Charles Nightingale, a British painter of the Victorian era. *Welcome Morsels* is a sentimental painting depicting a young girl feeding cabbage leaves to two goats.

The day my article appeared I had no sooner arrived at work than I received an irate phone call. The caller was miffed, to put it mildly, that I had written about a painting owned by his family, and that the newspaper had published an image of it, all of this without the family's permission. Soon afterwards I received another, very similar call.

Both callers were correct: they did own a *Welcome Morsels*. Both had relatives who had studied at the Canterbury College School of Art and as part of their training had made copies of *Welcome Morsels*. As Noah Charney notes in *The Art of Forgery*, 'copying has always been the way young artists learned their trade – copying or imitating another artist's style is only a crime if someone tries to pass off the copy as an original.' When copies by art students are handed on, as in these two cases, many later owners come to believe the painting is an original.

Copies can also be legitimately made as replicas of the real thing. In Rembrandt's time, copies were made for patrons who could not afford an original work. Usually these copies were made by an apprentice under the tutelage of the master painter. Not only did they provide works for collectors with modest budgets, they also provided a regular revenue stream for the artist. Today they are referred to as 'authorised replicas'.

There is a third type of copy, one that aims to make a statement. One example concerns a New Zealand artist, Heather Straka, and her exhibition *The Asian*, at Dunedin Public Art Gallery in 2010. Straka painted a portrait of a Shanghai poster girl from the 1920s or '30s, and then had fifty copies made by fifty different artists in Dafen Village, a gated settlement in China's Guangdong province. The Dafen story began in 1989 when an enterprising businessman displayed some paintings from village artists at a Hong Kong art fair and received a slew of orders. He hired more painters and in short order the town had 150 galleries and a thriving trade in fake artworks. Today around 5,000 artists live in Dafen, churning out replicas of paintings by everyone from Vincent Van Gogh – *Sunflowers* is the village's top seller – to Georgia O'Keeffe and Andy Warhol.

Straka's clever exhibition not only engaged visitors in trying to locate the original painting among the fifty on display, but stimulated conversations about copying, mass production and cultural attitudes. For instance, the young Asian woman in the portrait wears a tiki. Straka was making a point about Asian tourists buying tiki while holidaying in New Zealand and then taking them back to Asia, where they had probably been manufactured in the first place. And how original was Straka's own painting, drawing as it did on both poster art and the style of the Russian artist Vladimir Tretchikoff, whose 1950 painting *Chinese Girl* is one of the world's best-selling art prints?

ART HISTORIANS HAVE STRUGGLED to compile an exact catalogue of Goldie's work. Goldie copyists have muddied the waters: the popular New Zealand online auction website TradeMe has several

'Goldies' on offer at any given time, although most are very poor renderings. Some are distinctly humorous. As I write, one artist is offering a copy of Goldie's painting *A Good Joke*, with the subject's face changed to that of Sim.

But Goldie himself made things difficult. It is known that he copied numerous notable paintings, including *The Raft of the Medusa* by French painter Théodore Géricault, held at the Louvre, and *Portrait of a Burgomaster, after Rembrandt*, held by the Royal Gallery of Antwerp.[5] These and other fakes are held in private collections, indicating they were sold at some stage, perhaps as original artworks. But he also made multiple copies of his own works. There is no rule against an artist doing this and it was possibly Goldie's bread and butter. He probably felt no qualms, especially as the elderly models he had used at the beginning of the century were no longer alive when he copied their portraits in the 1930s.

All copies of artworks, good or bad, fraudulent or funny, raise issues of copyright. It seems Goldie himself was concerned about this. He tagged some of his works in sales catalogues 'copyright reserved', presumably in an effort, unsuccessful as it turned out, to stop them being reproduced.

In 2012 a muralist called Owen Dippie, using cans of spray paint, made a large copy on a wall of Goldie's 1902 portrait of a Ngāpuhi chieftainess, Ina Te Papatahi (sometimes called Ena Te Papatahi). The painting faces a public car park and toilets, and is often screened by parked cars. Dippie has signed it with his own name but in the style of Goldie's signature. The artist's signature indicates the work is a copy, but is this enough? In this case it probably is. According to the New Zealand Copyright Act 1994, a painting's copyright expires fifty years from the end of the year of the artist's death. In Goldie's case this means it has been legal since 1997 for anyone to produce copies of his work – as long as they do not pass them off as originals.

GOLDIE WAS PROLIFIC and to some extent criminals rely on this: the large quantity of 'Goldies' in circulation makes it easier for fakes to go unnoticed. And while the internet can hinder today's art criminal New Zealand does not have a register of stolen and missing works. However, the local art market is relatively small and contained, so trying to pass off a fake Goldie can be seen as an act of stupidity.

So, how can you tell if a 'Goldie' is genuine? I recommend you take some time to study the work closely – preferably with a magnifying glass. Goldie was a perfectionist and you should see great attention to detail: the hair, the skin, and the feathers of a cloak will all have different textural qualities, just as in real life. A characteristic was his incised lines of tā moko; these facial tattoos will appear like fine undulations. As Goldie often worked from photographs there may be other minute details.

Goldie painted on to a well-dried, thick, white-lead ground, then applied a layer of raw, dark yellowish-brown umber to soften the ground with a rounded brush. And he painted with confidence. In a genuine Goldie there will be no hesitation of brushwork: it will be ordered and uniform. If there is any smudginess (as sometimes seen in Sim's work) the work may not be authentic.

Goldie painted on both wood panels, often oak, and stretched canvases. If the canvas weave is thick and wide, as with hessian canvas, the painting is probably not genuine. And if the staples or tacks attaching the canvas to the stretcher look new, beware.

With authentification, the back of a work is just as important as the front. There may be an inscription, such as a dedication to an individual or a line about a gift, that can help. Exhibition labels are also telltale signs. Small stickers with numbers refer to those in exhibition catalogues and this information may be able to be checked. Be aware, though, that forgers commonly make up provenance and add bogus information to the backs of paintings.

Lastly, scrutinise the surface of the painting for tiny clues. Neil Roberts, the former senior curator at Christchurch Art Gallery, told me the last fake Goldie he saw had a visible fingerprint on the surface; it had been left by the impatient forger checking to see if the paint was dry – something Goldie would never have done.

IN 1933, WHEN HE CALLED A PORTRAIT *As Rembrandt would have painted the Maori*, Goldie may have been attempting to secure himself a dignified place in New Zealand art history. If this were the case, his effort was largely in vain. Much publicity about his work in recent years has focused on the crime surrounding it and the prices achieved at auction, while his position in the art canon has remained ambivalent. In 1997 and 1998 a large, impressive exhibition of his work was curated and toured by Auckland Art Gallery. The gallery's media release noted:

> Although much of [Goldie's] fame can be attributed to a history of vandalism, thefts, record-breaking prices and forgeries, perhaps the most interesting ingredient of the Goldie story is the dichotomy between the public and critical reception of his artwork, and how both have changed over time.

A typical contemporary view of Goldie's work is that of arts commentator Hamish Keith. In *The Big Picture*, Keith wrote:

> There is something poignant about this procession of melancholy elders, and while they are images that have a place in the story of New Zealand's colonial history they are not inspiring works of art.

Despite this, Goldie's work continues to impress viewers and collectors. This is no surprise: such highly polished representational paintings have wide appeal. Although he had trained in Paris during the early twentieth century, Goldie was no fan of modernism and continued to paint in a conservative hyper-realist style throughout his life.

His forger Karl Sim was similarly disdainful of modern art. In 1985 he pointed to a print of a self-portrait by celebrated New Zealand artist Frances Hodgkins and proclaimed to an interviewer, 'Look at that silly bitch behind you. What does it say? A self-portrait and look at it, there's a bloody shoe in her mouth.'

Meanwhile the Gibsons live in hope that one day their Goldie will be returned, although given the time that has elapsed since the theft it is hard to envisage this treasured painting ever making it back to Mosgiel. After the initial flurry of interest, the trail has gone cold. Bill Gibson noted that once the story slipped from the news, the police were 'conspicuous by their absence'. Perhaps, given the force's lack of resources and expertise for tracking art crime, this was inevitable.

Nor have the couple been compensated for their loss. The insurer, invoking the fine print of its policy, claimed the Gibsons were to blame. By hosting an open home run by a real estate agent they had invited people – including, by implication, potential thieves – into their house.

THREE

The Macchiaioli affair

IN 1994 DUNEDIN PUBLIC ART GALLERY purchased eight paintings that had been acquired in Italy in 1944 by Arthur Fraser. A bookkeeper from Caversham, Dunedin, Fraser had begun his working career as a machinist and gone on to work at New Zealand Wax Vesta Company, a factory manufacturing matchsticks. He was also an amateur artist and a member of the ambulance corps of the Territorial Army.

At the age of thirty-eight he signed up for war service, and as a private with the New Zealand Medical Corps Field Ambulance went on to serve in Africa, Fiji, Egypt and Italy. Thanks to the extensive documentation of this period, we know that during July and August 1944 the Field Ambulance Corps was based in Siena. It was here that Fraser purchased a suite of eight paintings by artists of the Macchiaioli School, a group based mainly in Florence during the second half of the nineteenth century and sometimes known as the 'Italian Impressionists'.

The paintings were:

Woman rocking a cradle (1881) by Odoardo Borrani (250 x 380 mm), oil on wood panel.

The baker's shop at Settignano (undated) by Telemaco Signorini (270 x 186 mm), oil on canvas.

Villa with approaching lane and trees (undated) by Telemaco Signorini (150 x 120 mm), oil on card.

Cavalryman with two horses (undated) by Giovanni Fattori (245 x 161 mm), oil on wood panel.

Road leading to buildings with bell tower (undated) by Guiseppe Abbati, (228 x 159 mm) oil on canvas on card.

Woman sitting by a window sewing (1872) by Silvestro Lega, (329 x 229 mm), oil on panel.

Study of a building against a stormy sky (undated), unknown artist, although signed lower right with an indecipherable signature, (145 x 215 mm), oil on wood panel.

Boy seated on chair with sketch pad (undated), unknown artist, (335 x 275 mm) watercolour.

At least one report has suggested that Fraser bought the paintings at a market, but it is more likely he acquired them at a commercial gallery. As an occasional artist himself, he possibly visited galleries during his times off duty. The purchase demonstrated not only his good taste in art but also his practicality: the works were small so they could be easily transported home to New Zealand.

Fraser was not the only New Zealand serviceman to bring home wartime souvenirs. The National Army Museum in Waiōuru contains a raft of war booty. One display case even contains relics from the 1944 Battle of Monte Cassino, including rosary beads, silverware, and an intricately carved wooden relief panel of acanthus leaves and putti. The label reads: 'Relics taken from the ruins of the

Monte Cassino Monastery' and provides no further provenance.

Fraser left Italy in April 1945 and was discharged from the army on July 24. He returned to the family home in Dunedin, where he lived to enjoy these souvenirs of his war years in Italy for two decades. When he died in 1964 his sister Dorothy Fraser inherited the paintings. Thirty years later, wanting to raise funds to leave an inheritance for the children of her other brother, David, she decided to offer them to the Dunedin Public Art Gallery. She was keen to keep the small collection of works together, and asked the gallery for the modest sum of $20,000. Less than five years later the five key works alone would be insured for $500,000.

THE DUNEDIN GALLERY JUMPED at the chance to acquire the Macchiaioli collection. Not only would the paintings add to the gallery's already substantial international holdings, they would enhance and provide context for the other Italian works in its collection, in particular eleven works by Girolamo Pieri Pecci Ballati Nerli. Nerli was an Italian artist who settled in Dunedin in the 1890s and became an art teacher to the young Frances Hodgkins and her sister Isabel. Before emigrating to New Zealand he had worked on the fringe of the Macchiaioli School.

The word 'macchia' means spots of colour and refers to the group's loose handling and application of paint; they used these spots or blobs of paint to create a fresh, sparkling quality. Many works, especially the landscapes and town scenes, were painted outdoors working directly from nature, a novel method at the time.

The paintings' fresh sense of immediacy would add new vibrancy to the gallery's collection as well as prestige – no other public art gallery in New Zealand or Australia had comparable works. They would also increase the gallery's ability to borrow works from other museums for exhibitions. As the director, John McCormack, told the *Otago Daily Times*, 'If you don't have major works in your own holdings, it's impossible to borrow.'

It had been five decades since Fraser had brought the paintings to Dunedin from Italy. In an interview with the *Otago Daily Times* in 2008, John Timmins, the gallery's collections manager, said he had researched the provenance of the collection as best he could prior to the purchase, and 'had also established, with a paper trail, that they had been bought legitimately by Mr Fraser in Siena in 1943 and legally exported'. Establishing provenance would not have been helped by the fact the paintings were not in their original frames: it was possible Fraser had removed them when leaving Italy in 1945 as low-ranking personnel had a limited luggage allowance.

IN 1996, TWO YEARS AFTER the acquisition, the gallery received a request from the Pananti Gallery in Florence. The gallery was curating an exhibition of 132 paintings of the Macchiaioli School and wished to borrow Dunedin's five key works: *Woman rocking a cradle*, *The baker's shop at Settignano*, *Villa with approaching trees*, *Cavalryman with two horses* and *Woman sitting by a window sewing*. As the Dunedin gallery had made it known internationally that it had acquired the Fraser works, it was a reasonable request. The exhibition, *I Macchiaioli, Nuovi Contributi* (The Macchiaioli, New Contributions), would run from October 4, 1997 to July 6, 1998.

At the time most New Zealand galleries had little experience of lending works internationally. John Timmins took advice from New Zealand Customs and the National Art Gallery about the documentation necessary to ensure the works would not incur customs levies when entering Italy and exiting at the end of the loan period. A document known as an ATA Carnet, suitable for the temporary export of goods overseas and valid for one year, was sought. This would ensure customs clearance in Italy and no payment of duty when the paintings returned to New Zealand. Following advice from the Ministry of Cultural Affairs, two extra clauses were added to the loan agreement with the Pananti Gallery: New Zealand law would apply, and all disputes and differences that might arise between the parties would be referred to arbitration in accordance with the New Zealand Arbitration Act 1908.

With all measures in place the agreement was signed in June 1997. Timmins felt comfortable he had done everything necessary to make the transaction failproof and safe. The consignment, accompanied by a senior member of the gallery's staff, departed for Italy on September 12.

At Rome airport on September 13 the staff member was stopped by Italian Customs. The works had to be cleared before the final leg of their journey to Florence, and this would inevitably mean a delay. It was two weeks before staff at Dunedin Public Art Gallery discovered the delivery had not gone according to plan: on September 27 they learned that the works were still with Italian Customs, and not at the Pananti Gallery as they had assumed.

The staff member had handed over the ATA Carnet to Customs, so the gallery now had no documentation about the paintings.[6] Soon afterwards it received some disturbing news: the works were listed on a register of stolen paintings, *Treasures Untraced: An Inventory of the Italian Art Treasures Lost During the Second World War*. Work on *Treasures Untraced* had begun in earnest in the 1950s, led by Rodolfo Siviero, an art historian and member of the Italian Resistance who had been collecting titbits of art-related intelligence for years. He would become famous for his efforts to locate Italian artworks stolen by the Nazis, gaining the nickname '007 of art'. Siviero felt strongly that all the stolen works should be returned to Italy. Luisa Morozzi, an art historian and the co-author of *Treasures Untraced*, who was based at the airport, had recognised the paintings and had them seized.

In a short time what was to have been a simple delivery of five paintings had escalated to a complex and volatile situation. In due course the Dunedin Public Art Gallery was told the paintings would be released for the Pananti exhibition and the Italian court would institute no penal action, but the descendants of Professor Cino Vitta, the paintings' original owner, had been contacted. Civil action was likely.

WHAT WAS TO BECOME KNOWN as 'The Macchiaioli Affair' had come about through a series of unfortunate events. Private Fraser had purchased the works in Italy in good faith. His sister Dorothy had sold them to Dunedin Public Art Gallery for very little in an admirably philanthropic gesture. But should the paintings have been offered for sale in 1944? The answer is no. They were stolen goods, looted by the Nazis or another party keen to make a profit and/or do harm to Professor Vitta, a prominent leader of Florence's Jewish community.

Vitta owned thirty-two Macchiaioli paintings and they were among his prized possessions. In 1938, following the introduction of anti-Semitic laws in Mussolini's Italy, he had moved the paintings to a house on his farm estate and asked one of his tenants, who worked on the farm, to secure the building. He and his wife Emma had then sought refuge in a mental asylum in Siena for the duration of the war, using false documents that certified them as insane. At the end of the war Vitta visited the farm and was distressed to find his precious artworks had disappeared.

The looting of artworks that took place under the Nazis is well documented. A failed artist himself, Hitler planned to build a magnificent art museum at Linz in Austria, to be filled with works that he would personally select. The public collections in Germany were not a match for those found in Italy. In May 1938 Hitler visited the Uffizi Gallery in Florence with Mussolini. Much to Mussolini's annoyance the tour lasted four hours as Hitler eyed up what he would like for his museum.

Once organised confiscations began in earnest during the war, many public and domestic art collections were looted, both for the Linz project and for the private collections of Hitler and Göring, one of Hitler's right-hand men. All Jewish property became fair game. By the time German troops reached Italy in September 1943 they had already helped themselves to around 60,000 artworks in France and 59,000 in Poland.

Lynn Nicholas, in her seminal text *The Rape of Europa*, gives a sense of the scale of Hitler's operation in France alone. 'Between April 1941 and July 1944,' she writes, '4,174 cases, which filled 138 boxcars and contained at least 22,000 lots, were shipped out to the Reich.'

Although an effort was made in Italy to protect some collections, there was organised looting and destruction. Even when works were moved and hidden to try to protect them, lack of care around transport and storage meant many were damaged. In some instances works were saved only because they were too large and complex for the Nazis to move. This was the case with Benvenuto Cellini's sixteenth-century bronze sculpture *Perseus with the Head of Medusa*, which still stands in Florence's Piazza Della Signoria.[7]

Works were often taken en masse, to be sorted later. Those that did not fit Hitler's curatorial mandate for Linz, or the other museums for which he was 'shopping', were sold or destroyed. It is possible the works in Cino Vitta's collection were surplus to requirements and sold to a local art dealer, where Fraser saw and purchased eight of them.

In 1945 Vitta provided a complete catalogue of his missing Macchiaioli paintings to an official body, the Committee for the Recovery of Stolen Italian Art, which had been set up to search for lost works. For five decades nothing was heard, until in 1997 Italian Customs officials contacted Vitta's grandsons, Johanan and Nathanel Vitta, and advised them of the five artworks from New Zealand that had surfaced at Rome airport. For the Vitta family the discovery of the works may have rekindled the hurt felt over the original theft. Born and raised in Jerusalem, Vitta's grandsons Johanan and Nathanel Vitta had never seen the paintings their grandfather had loved.

WHEN THE CIVIL ACTION BEGAN in a Florence court, the Dunedin Public Art Gallery was asked through Interpol to prove ownership of the works. It produced Private Fraser's New Zealand Defence Force file; this contained a 1998 request from the gallery for Fraser's wartime records, showing it had tried to establish where he had been stationed during the war.

The Vitta family, who had expected the paintings to be returned to them without argument, were disappointed when in December the court pronounced the Dunedin Public Art Gallery to be the lawful owner. The family immediately appealed the court's decision and also initiated an investigation aimed at charging the gallery with having purchased the paintings illegally.

As time wore on it became clear that trying to get the paintings returned to Dunedin was becoming ever more arduous and costly, and was possibly doomed to failure. By late January 1998 the Pananti Gallery exhibition was over and the paintings were back in Rome. The Dunedin City Council, as the local body responsible for the gallery, was having to pay growing sums of money to lawyers in both Florence and Rome. Understandably anxious, the gallery staff came up with a plan. If they could get the paintings to London with the assistance of the New Zealand Embassy in Rome, they would be a step closer to bringing them home. Alas, this was not how it would play out.

In May 1999 Johanan Vitta said he and his brother both adored the works, especially Odoardo Borrani's *Woman rocking a cradle*, and wanted their children to inherit them as part of their family's heritage. They were prepared to pay the Dunedin Public Art Gallery the original 1994 purchase price of $20,000 and possibly share the works. On July 8, 1999 a settlement was reached. The five paintings would be split between the two parties, with the apportioning based on current valuations. The Vittas would receive *Woman rocking a cradle* and Telemaco Signorini's *The baker's shop at Settignano*, together valued later at approximately $500,000.[8] Provision was made for unimpeded export of the remaining works to New Zealand and the dropping of the impending criminal charges.

From New Zealand's perspective this was a reasonably good outcome. Achieving the return of three of the paintings had cost the Dunedin City Council around $170,000, most of it in legal fees, but even more costly and lengthy litigation had been avoided: Dunedin Public Art Gallery had been advised that if it didn't accept the settlement a final decision could take up to eight years. Meanwhile, though, this major gallery had lost two significant works. Some people, including the gallery's curator Peter Entwisle, believed a corrupt Italian legal system had made it easy for the Vittas to acquire works that were technically owned by the gallery, something the family had more or less admitted.

Almost immediately after the settlement the brothers put their two works up for auction, perhaps to cover legal costs, or so funds could be distributed between the two of them in accordance with Jewish rules of inheritance. In the catalogue of Farsetti, the auction house, *Woman rocking a cradle* had a before-sale estimate of £80,000 and *The baker's shop at Settignano* £43,000. In early 2007 one of the company's principals, Sonia Farsetti, wrote in a blog entry that the two paintings had sold for double the estimated price.[9] In fact *Woman rocking the cradle* had fetched an astonishing €205,000.

In late 2014 *The baker's shop at Settignano* sold again, this time for €120,000.[10] Fraser had paid just 200 lire – about four days' pay – for it.

MUCH HAS BEEN MADE of the Dunedin Public Art Gallery's failure to search the *Art Loss Register*, the private database of lost and stolen art, antiques and collectables that was established in London in 1990, before purchasing the Macchiaioli paintings. John Timmins recalled that in all the correspondence about the potential acquisition no international expert had ever suggested searching this register. When I checked the register myself, I found the Macchiaioli works had not been added until 1995, so even if a search had been carried out in 1994 nothing would have been found. Timmins also noted that at the time the gallery had purchased the Fraser collection it held few international publications and had little or no access to art media that profiled cases of looted art.

In *Treasures Untraced* all thirty-two of Professor Cino Vitta's Macchiaioli works carry this notation:

> Stolen by Nazi troops from Mr. Limi's home who stored the painting at S. Martino a Cozzi, outlying district of S. Donato in Poggio, in the parish of Tavarnelle Val di Pesa (Florence) in Spring 1944.

The 1956 volume of New Zealand's official war history, *New Zealand Medical Services in the Middle East and Italy*, shows that servicemen, including medics, were in this area in July 1944. As the works were stolen some time in the spring – March to May – the timeframe fits.

It has been established that approximately 516,000 individual works of art were looted in Europe during the Second World War. The process of gathering and listing all the relevant information has taken over half a century and is still ongoing. Today a number of international agreements attempt to regulate and encourage repatriation of Nazi-confiscated art. In 1998 Germany and forty-three other countries agreed to the Washington Principles, under which they would investigate the provenance of artworks in their public collections, publicise any shown to have been stolen, and encourage a just and fair solution to conflicting claims of ownership. New Zealand did not become a party to the Washington Principles, possibly because Nazi-confiscated art had not been a major issue in the country.

Today purchasers of artworks, especially major galleries and other public institutions, are seen as having a moral duty to to carry out due diligence and rigorously check legal titles, especially to works that may have any connection with the Second World War and/or have been Jewish property. The *Art Loss Register* suggests that even if legal title has been attributed to the buyer, it may be morally correct to return the works to their original owners or their descendants.

The Macchiaioli Affair grabbed the attention of the media, both in New Zealand and abroad. The *Otago Daily Times* followed the litigation closely as Dunedin residents awaited the outcome with interest and concern. *The Art Newspaper*, an international monthly publication, published an article on the case in 1998 entitled 'Five Macchiaioli in the business of war'. The writer endorsed the work of Rodolfo Siviero in 'discovering' stolen Italian art and seeing the return of works thought to have been lost indefinitely. 'But of course we must kindle the disputes, start diplomatic negotiations,' the paper added. 'For some it is much easier to forget Siviero.' The *New Zealand Listener* covered the story in May 1999 and included an image of Silvestro Lega's beautiful painting *Woman sitting by a window sewing*, guaranteed to tug at the heartstrings.

In the years since the settlement, the Macchiaioli affair has not been covered up by Dunedin Public Art Gallery, but it has certainly not been given undue exposure. The gallery's 125th anniversary exhibition in 2010, and the associated book *Beloved: Works from the Dunedin Public Art Gallery*, included in the more than two hundred key works from the gallery's collection *Woman sitting by a window sewing*, but there was no mention of its chequered past. Peter Entwisle, reviewing the book in the *Otago Daily Times*, mentioned this omission with surprise: the Macchiaioli paintings had been 'a matter of extensive international publicity and one of the most striking acquisitions of recent decades'.

In his 2008 book *Stolen: The Gallery of Missing Masterpieces*, Canadian writer Jonathan Webb suggested the gallery had been lax. 'No one … had been following developments in the art world regarding the recovery of Holocaust art. The Dunedin [Public Art Gallery] was not being especially careful, as other galleries were beginning to be, of works that might have changed hands in the period from 1933 to 1945.'

David Swartz, president of New Zealand's Jewish Council, was of the same opinion. In April 1998 he told *The New Zealand Herald*: 'A gallery that buys things from soldiers who have been in a country that's been occupied and had its Jewish population murdered or deported, either they are naïve or acting scurrilously to just buy something without checking on it.'

Interestingly, however, it has never been proved that the Macchiaioli works were stolen by the Nazis. The place where they were stored could have been raided by German troops, who then decided against keeping the paintings and sold them off to a local dealer. The paintings could equally well have been stolen by Italians.

JOHN TIMMINS HAS DESCRIBED the entire Dunedin episode as fraught from the outset. For the gallery's staff the loss of the paintings was a damning blow and they felt underrepresented in the Italian legal system. Both the gallery and the city council were well out of their depth, 'country cousins caught in the headlights', and it was, in Timmins' view, only their lawyer Joe Butler who managed to save three of the paintings for Dunedin. However, this was an unusual case, with little or no precedents in the country, and would have challenged most local bodies. In approving the loans to the Pananti Gallery the gallery had acted in good faith. Lending works is seen as part of the core business of a public art gallery and there have to be very good reasons to turn down such requests provided conditions – such as the environment in which the works will be displayed, the transport to and from the borrowing gallery, the insurance, and the staffing – meet recognised standards.

All parties in the Macchiaioli affair can be seen as both losers and winners. Few would deny that returning lost art to Italy, especially works stolen during the Second World War, is justice in action. To fail to do so would be, as Susanna Agnelli, the country's Minister of Foreign Affairs said in 1995, to deny Italy of its culture. The Vitta family regained two long-lost paintings, but they lost three others they had hoped would be repatriated. Legal expenses also cost them dearly.

The Dunedin Public Art Gallery, for its part, lost two recently acquired works, and as a result New Zealand art-lovers were no longer able to view Fraser's entire collection of Macchiaioli paintings, with their intriguing wartime story. The gallery also paid large legal fees defending the case in court. However, it still had six other Macchiaioli paintings, for which it had paid very little in the first place. And the provenance of the three 'returned' paintings gained a new chapter: that the works had been fought for so openly added to their value and interest.

Yet there remain unanswered questions. With the exception of assistance from Luisa Morozzi, the art historian who was based at Rome Airport, all my requests to Italian authorities for information met with silence. The most significant question concerns the loan request from the Pananti Gallery. In an effort to try and find more information about the paintings, the Dunedin Public Art Gallery had advertised the fact it had acquired them. Was the request from the Pananti Gallery an innocent one? Or had someone in Italy checked and found the paintings could have been stolen during the war and forged a plan to borrow and then seize them when they arrived in Italy? It seems a surprising coincidence that the loan request was made in 1996, just months after the publication of *Treasures Untraced*.

There is some evidence to confirm this suspicion. A story about the artist Silvestro Lega in Italian journal *Il Corriere Nazionale* of July 11, 2015 suggests that Piero Pananti, the gallery owner who requested the loan, and Michele Miulli, an art expert with the Italian police, had searched the database of the Carabinieri Department for the Protection of Cultural Heritage and discovered the Macchiaioli works listed as missing around the same time the loan request reached the Dunedin Public Art Gallery.[11] In addition, of the eight works held in Dunedin only the five most valuable were requested. Did the other three not fit the curatorial criteria for the exhibition – or was it felt they were not valuable enough to be worth pursuing?

It is not clear whether the Vitta heirs, who stood to benefit materially from the paintings' return, knew of the gallery's loan request. During the legal proceedings they claimed not to have done so, describing the telephone call from Rome's airport as a surprise. Yet when they received the 'adored' paintings they immediately put them up for auction.

And then there was the role of Luisa Morozzi. Was she particularly astute in noticing the paintings, or had she been tipped off that they were arriving? When I contacted Morozzi in 2014 she was helpful but did not elucidate. She did tell me that as at

December that year, of the 2,356 items listed in *Treasures Untraced* only three or four had been recovered, including the two Macchiaioli works.

Perhaps the final word should be left to Johanan Vitta, who told the *New Zealand Listener*:

> Arthur Fraser seems to have been an admirable fellow. … As he had come to Italy to liberate it from the Nazis and fascists, we feel that if he'd known the paintings were stolen because our family had to flee racial persecution he wouldn't have bought them. Or if he learnt about it later he would have given them back to the family.

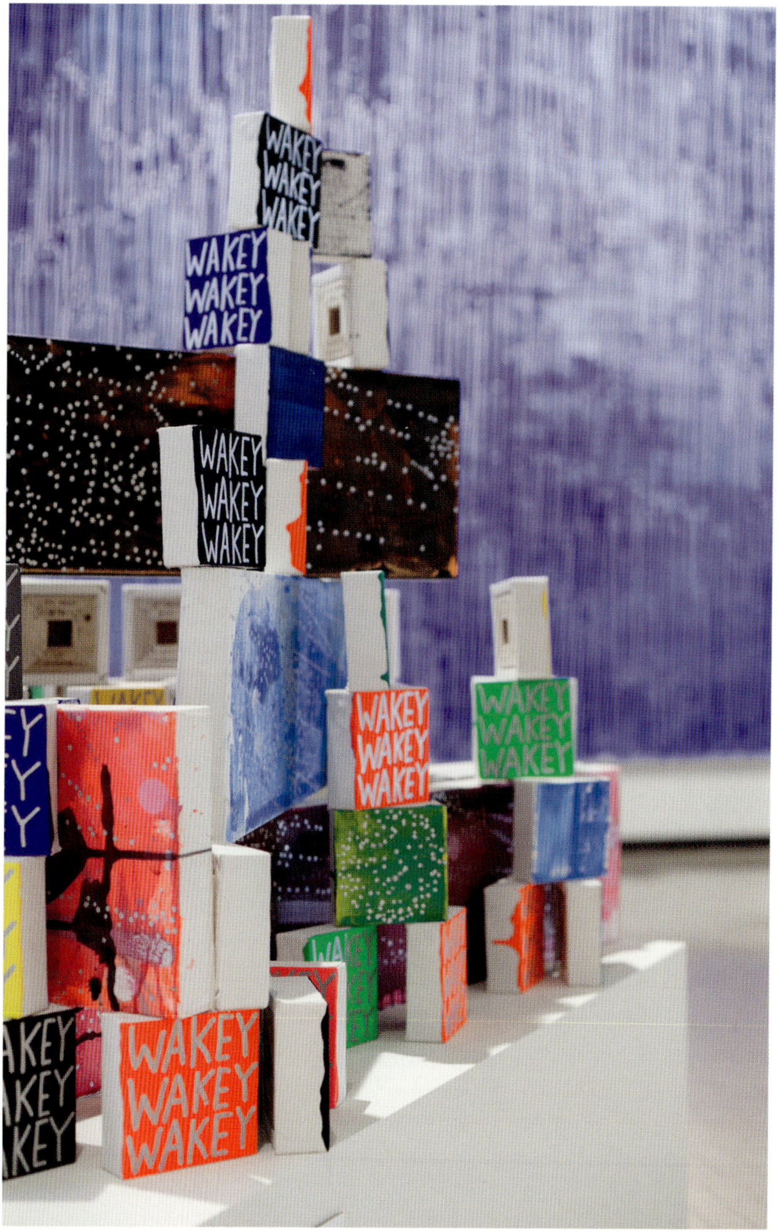

Wakey, Wakey, Wakey, an installation of 113 works by John Reynolds, inspired by a visit to the Kermadec Islands. While on display in Tauranga Art Gallery Toi Tauranga in 2012 two canvases were stolen. *Kate Whitley photograph*

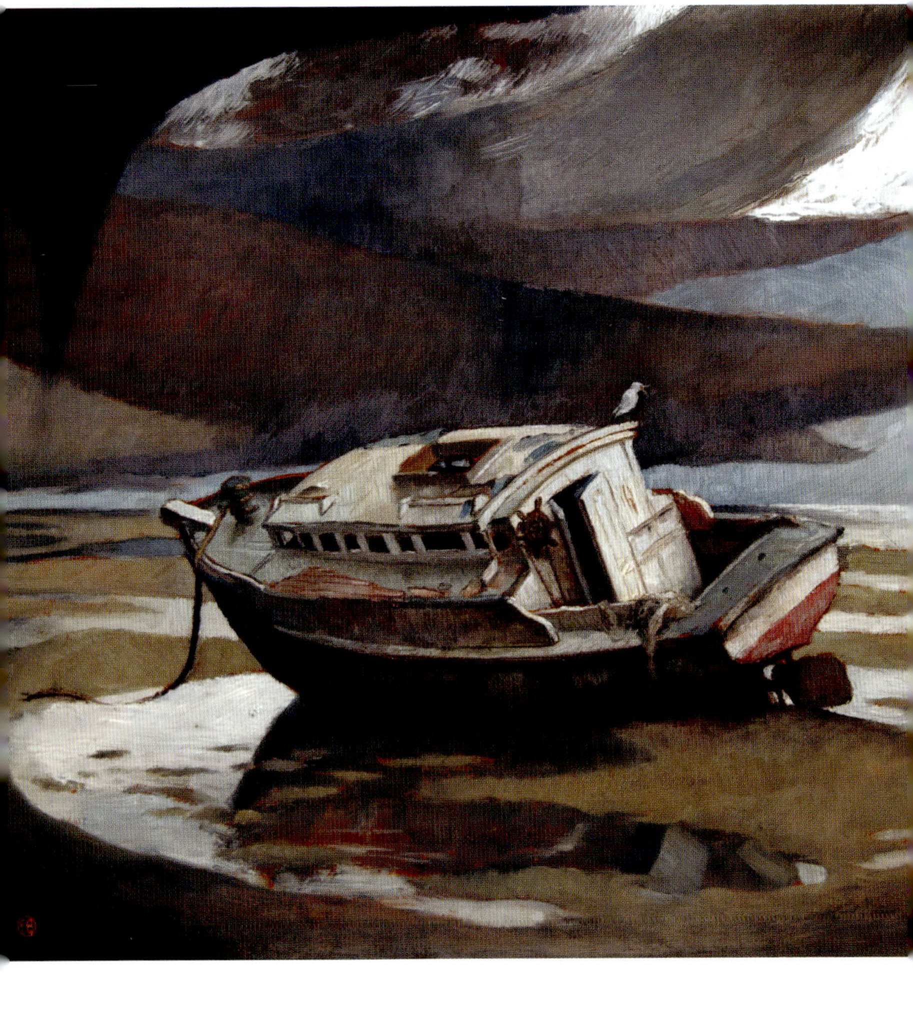

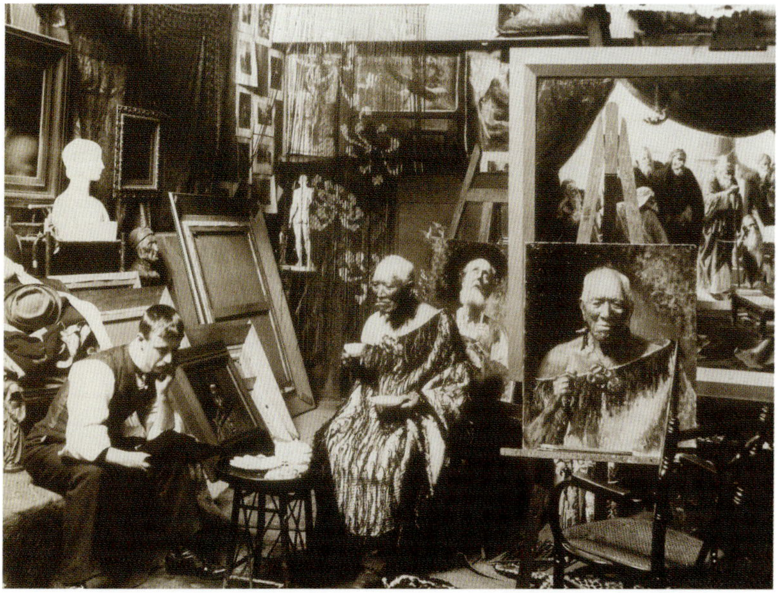

LEFT *Derelict* by Edward Bullmore, painted in 1957 when the artist was twenty-four and not long out of art school. *Tauranga City Council/Marianna Bullmore*

ABOVE C.F. Goldie in his Auckland studio with Waikato leader Wiremu Patara Te Tuhi, 1901. A painting of Te Tuhi sits on an easel in the foreground. Goldie used many Māori as sitters; today his portraits are sometimes seen as irreplacable records of ancestors. *Museum of New Zealand Te Papa Tongarewa*

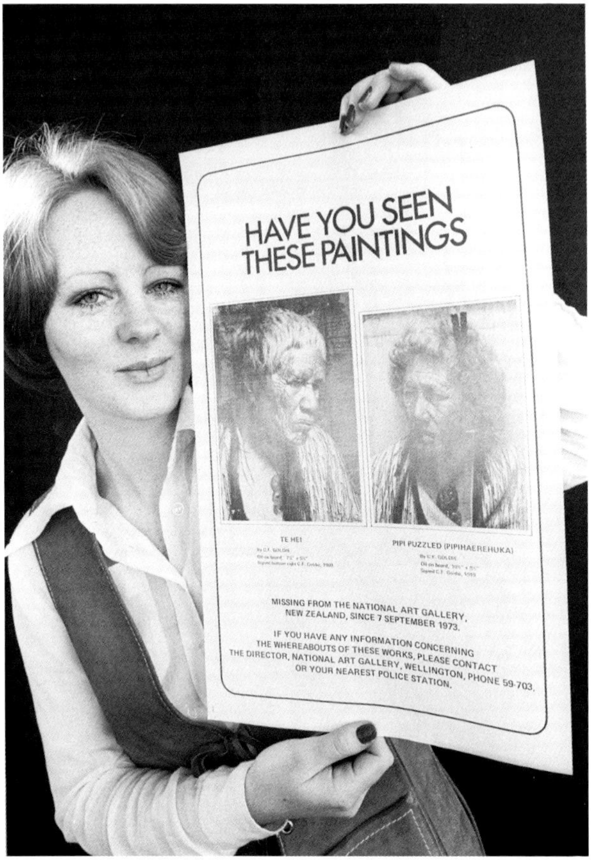

Evening Post reporter Catherine Perry holds a poster seeking return of two Goldie paintings which vanished mysteriously from the National Art Gallery in September 1973. The poster was distributed to police and auction houses in New Zealand and worldwide.

Alexander Turnbull Library EP/1973/4353/24A-F

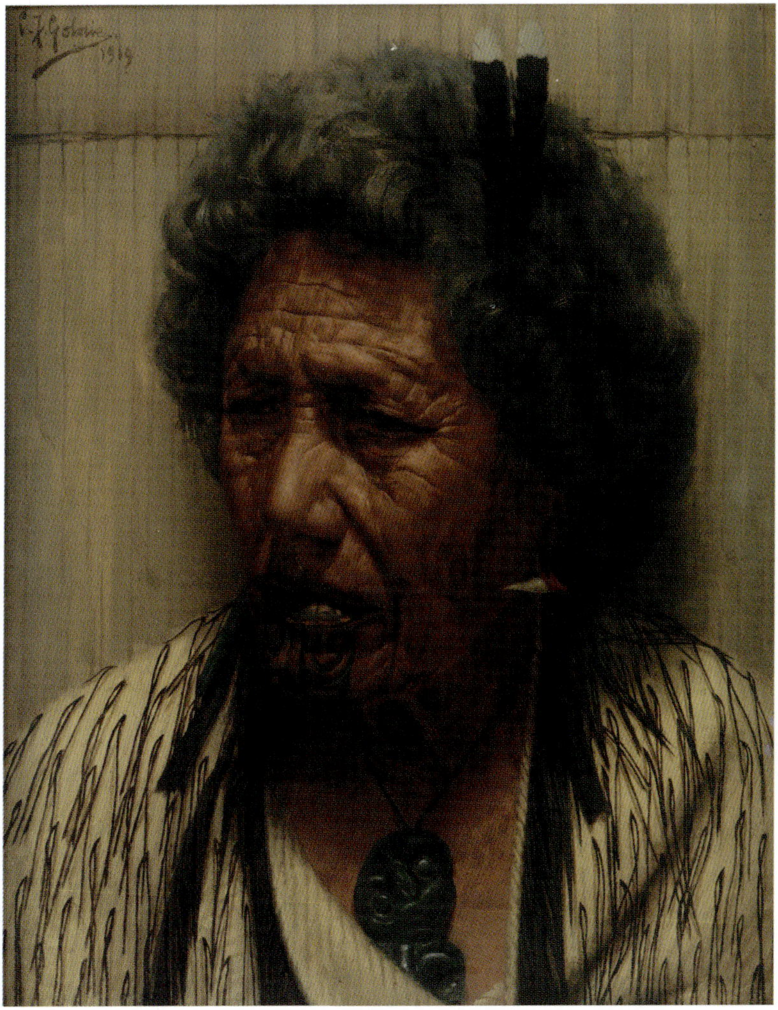

Pipi Puzzled, a 1919 portrait of Pipi Haerehuka of Ngāti Whakaue that was one of two Goldie paintings stolen from the National Art Gallery. At the time each was valued at $6,000. *Museum of New Zealand Te Papa Tongarewa*

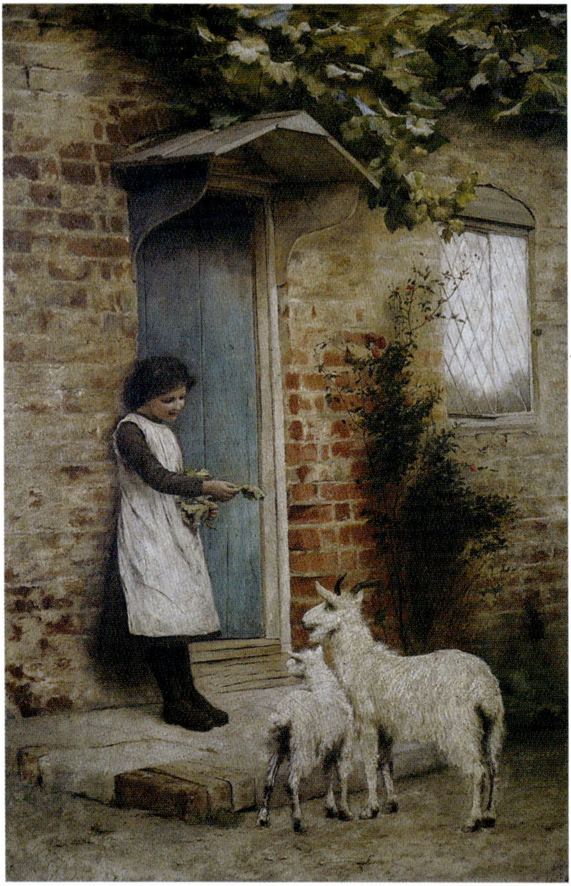

Welcome Morsels by British painter Leonard Charles Nightingale. When a story about the painting, held by the Robert McDougall Art Gallery in Christchurch appeared in *The Press*, two indignant callers claimed the painting belonged to them. *Christchurch Art Gallery Te Puna o Waiwhetu*

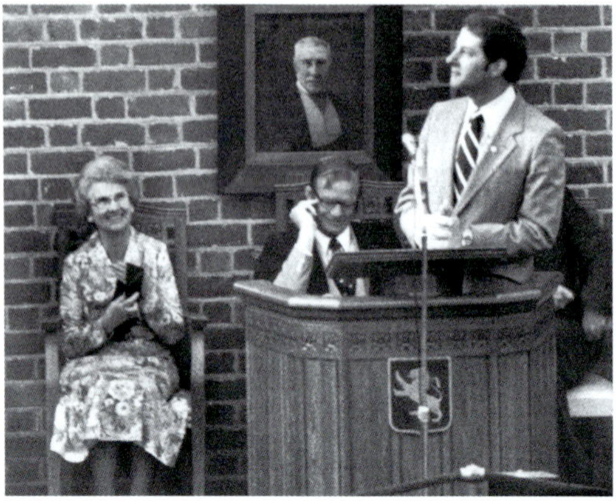

In February 1987 four artworks were stolen from the collection of Auckland Grammar School, including *Portrait of Sir George Grey* by Louis John Steele, an oil painting seen here hanging in the school hall. After arriving from England in 1886, Steele painted many prominent Aucklanders and also taught C.F. Goldie. *Auckland Grammar School*

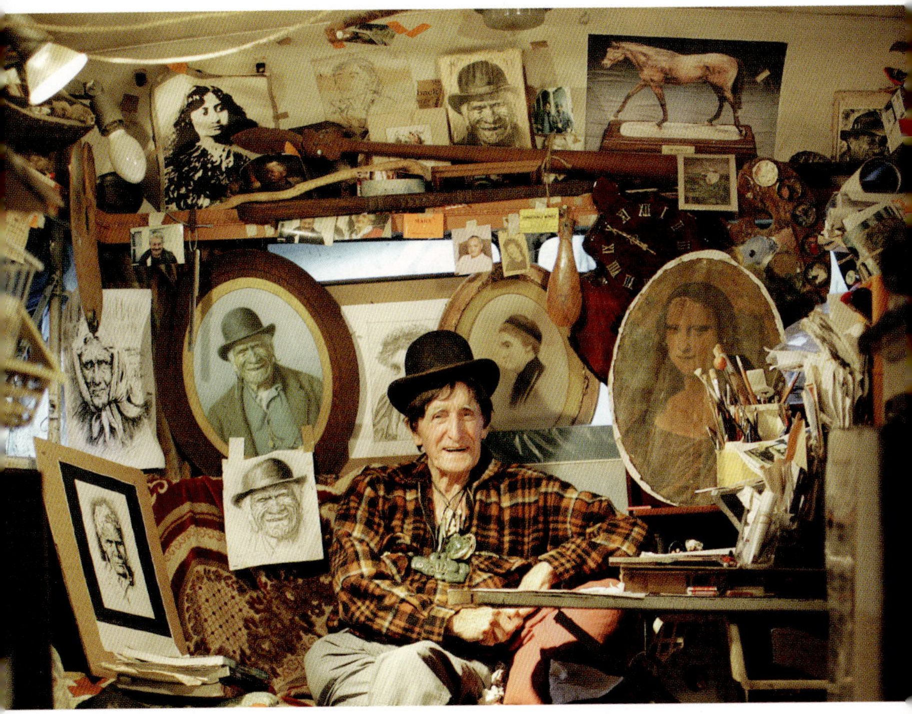

Karl Sim, aka Carl Feodor Goldie, at his Hatfields Beach retreat. A copy of Goldie's portrait *Te Aho-o-te-Rangi Wharepu, Ngati Mahuta* is on his right, and a fake *Mona Lisa* on his left. *David White photograph, Fairfax New Zealand*

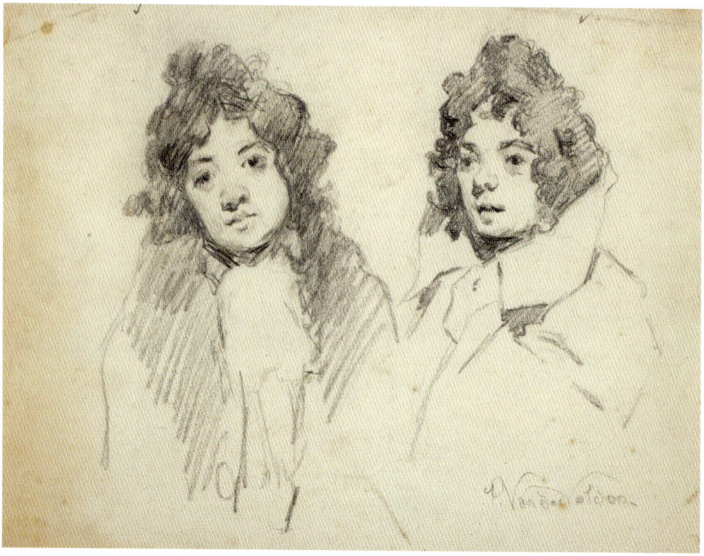

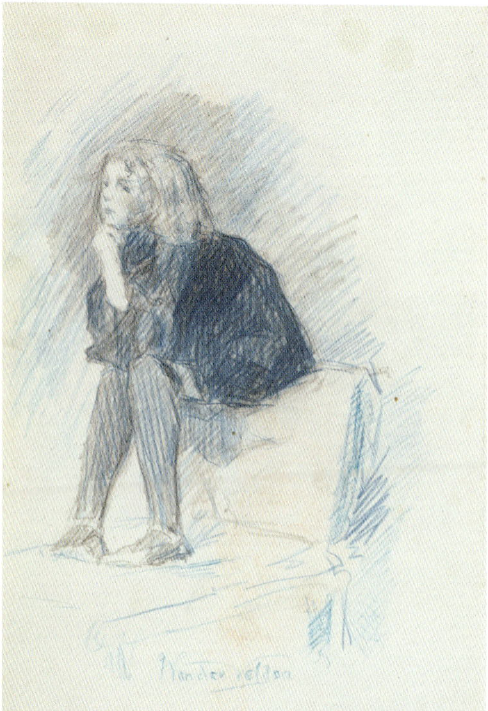

Two of the more than thirty-six forged sketches by Karl Sim purchased by the National Art Gallery as genuine works by Dutch-born artist Petrus van der Velden. During Sim's trial, a forensic document examiner not that all signatures on the drawin shared characteristics with Sim's handwriting.
ABOVE Two head studies of a young girl.
LEFT Study of a young boy.
Museum of New Zealand Te Papa Tongarew

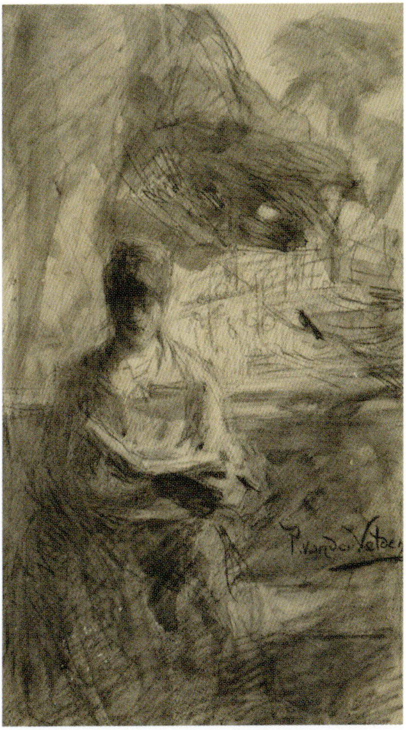

Genuine sketches by van der Velden.
RIGHT Woman reading, c. 1872.
BELOW Man reading, c. 1873.
Museum of New Zealand Te Papa Tongarewa

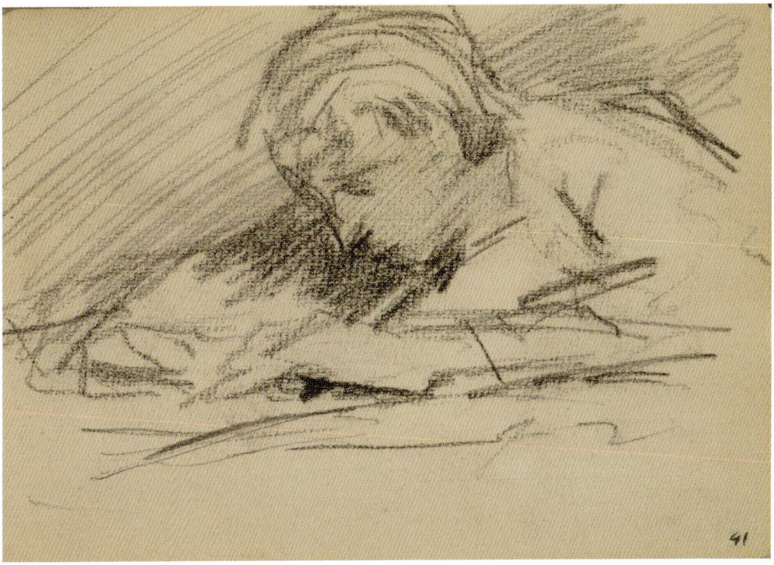

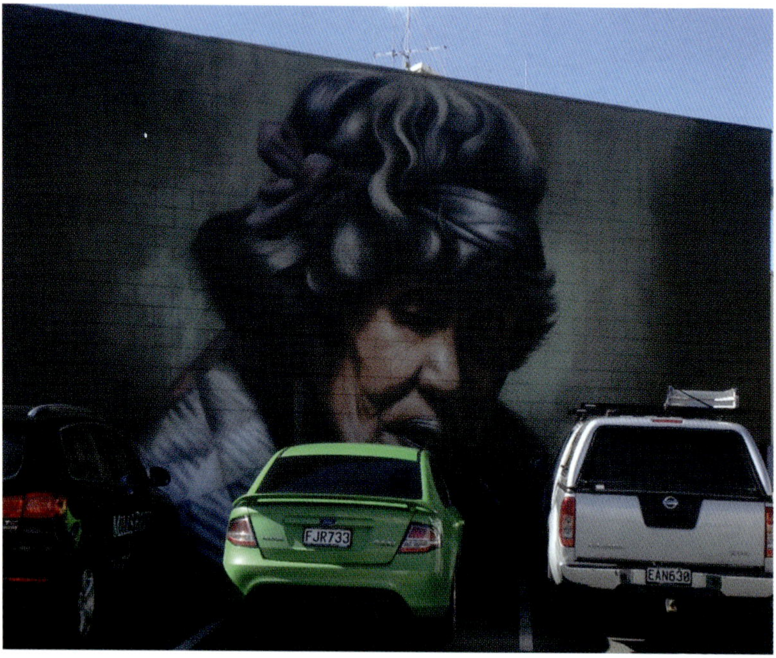

ABOVE A 2012 copy of Goldie's 1902 portrait of a Ngāpuhi chieftainess, Ina Te Papatahi, by muralist Owen Dippie, and signed by him in Goldie's 'font', on a wall fronting a car park in Tauranga. *Daniel du Bern photograph*

RIGHT Woman sitting by a window sewing, an 1872 oil by Silvestro Lega purchased by Dunedin Public Art Gallery in 1994. This painting and four others of the Italian Macchiaioli School would become the focus of an international tug-of-war. *Dunedin Public Art Gallery*

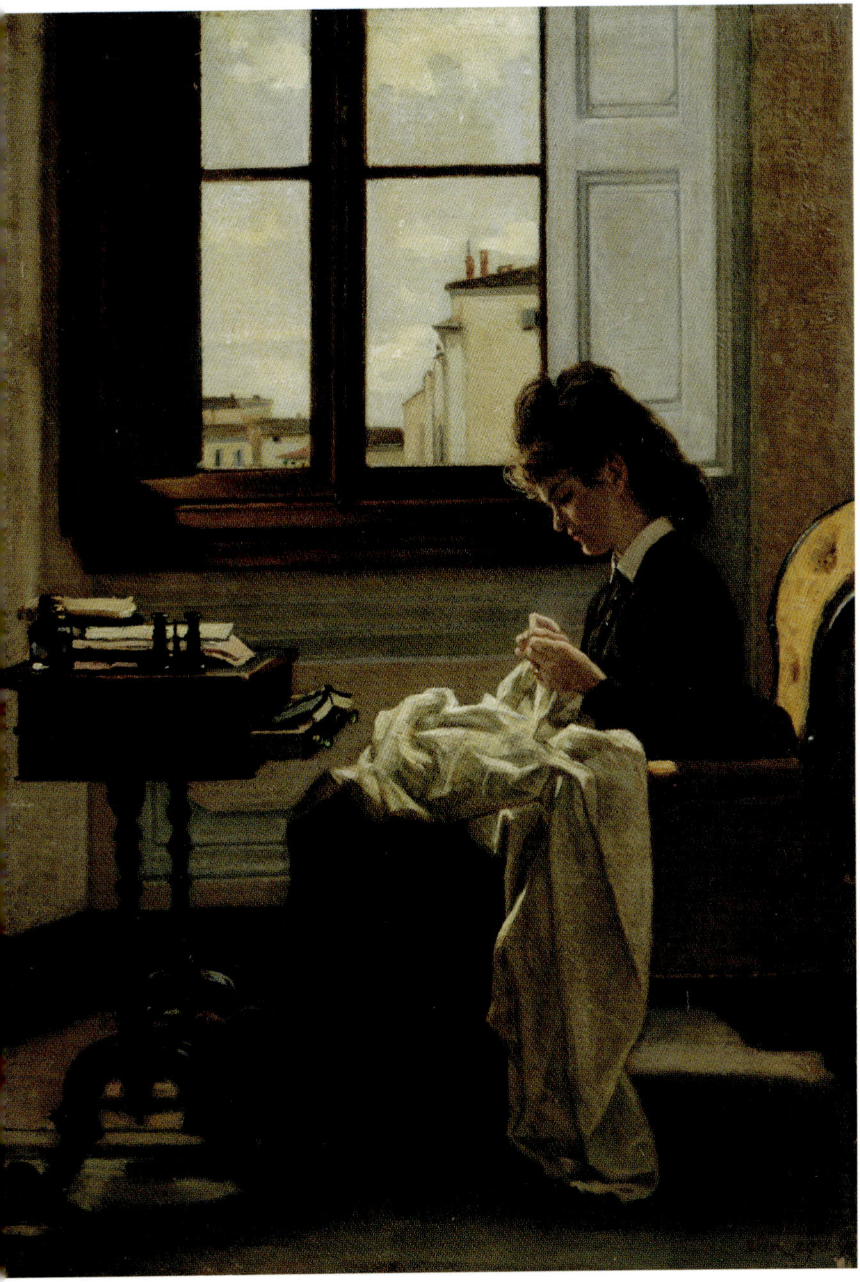

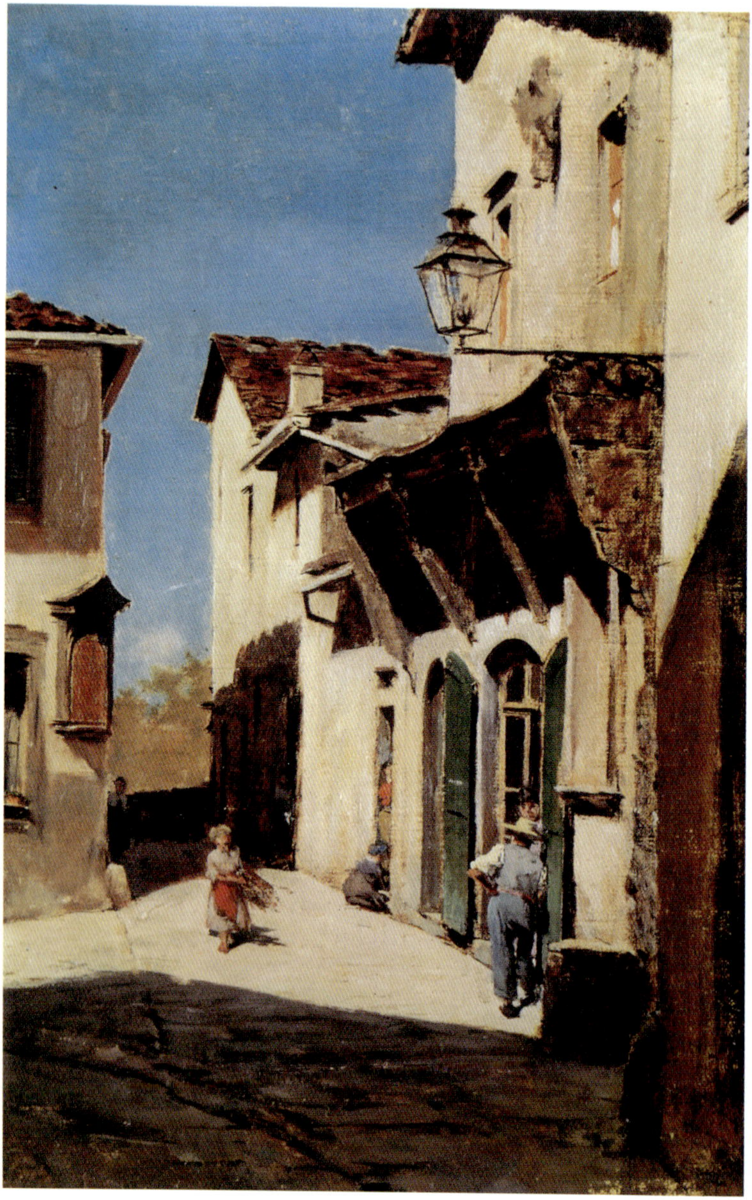

The baker's shop at Settignano, an undated oil on canvas by Telemaco Signorini, was one of thirty-two Macchiaioli paintings owned by a prominent member of Florence's Jewish community and stolen during the Second World War. The painting's innocent purchase by a New Zealand soldier in 1944 would lead to a major art scandal fifty years later.

FOUR

Caveat emptor

THE TERM CAVEAT EMPTOR – let the buyer beware – should ring in the ears of everyone considering an art purchase. It pays to examine the work in detail, including its condition and provenance. In some instances information will be left out of sales catalogues and it is up to the buyer to make enquiries and try to fill in the gaps. Although there is stiff competition among art dealers and auction houses in New Zealand today, and this has led to increasingly professional attitudes and presentation, there are still those who deceive purchasers. The following three incidents, involving major New Zealand artists, illustrate what can go wrong when a buyer is too trusting.

Peter Siddell's brushwork

IN 2012 THE TAURANGA ART GALLERY decided to exhibit a suite of works from private collections of Friends of the Gallery. Exhibitions like this are a popular way to showcase works that are seldom seen publicly.

A painting by the artist Peter Siddell was put forward for selection. The painting's owner, Mary Hackett, was both a Friend of the Gallery and a trustee. The work, called *Orange Glass* and dated 2005, measured 280 x 400 mm and was in many ways a Siddell classic, featuring a colonial villa perched among the lush vegetation of an Auckland hillside. I could see why Hackett, a former Aucklander, had been attracted to this delightful painting. And there was a family connection: her sister was a friend of the artist, who had died in 2011, and his wife and fellow artist Sylvia Siddell.

When staff collected the work, the gallery's technician, Matt Henry, was very taken with the painting – and a little apprehensive. He was particularly interested in the smoothness of the surface. An artist himself, he was struck by both the the lack of visible brushwork and rendering of minute detail.

Given his suspicions, the gallery felt it was prudent to seek the opinion of professional conservators. With the owner's permission, *Orange Glass* was taken to experts at the Auckland Art Gallery. Ultraviolet lights have the ability to quickly show whether a painting really is a painting in the true sense of the term, or simply a manufactured copy. Almost immediately the conservators confirmed that the Siddell work was a digital copy. Some brushwork had been added in the area of the sky and down the left-hand side of the canvas. Siddell's signature had also been painted on.

When the work was removed from the frame, it was evident it was not a stretched canvas. Instead the image had been printed on to a piece of canvas, which had then been cut to fit an existing wooden frame. The frame was not quite the right size, hence the addition of paint down the left-hand side. The canvas had been neatly wrapped around the wooden frame and fixed with staples.

Orange Glass had been sold as a genuine oil painting. When the gallery told Mary Hackett what it had found, she contacted Peter Siddell's family. Their reply was that Siddell had been going through an experimental phase in his artistic practice when he made the work, and had also been undergoing treatment for a brain tumour. Expressing some embarrassment, they immediately refunded the entire purchase price.

Subsequent research revealed that Siddell had sold digital prints of several of his paintings through a store in the Auckland suburb of Mt Eden for $120 each, a reasonable price for a print. In 2009 Mary Hackett had purchased a print like one of these directly from the Siddells for $7,500. This was a hard lesson: she had acquired the work from a supposedly reputable source and so had not questioned its authenticity. Why would she? Yet she been duped into buying a fraud. With printing processes becoming increasingly sophisticated, copies will continue to infiltrate art markets and cases such as this will become increasingly common.

Toss Woollaston's 'collaborator'

THE REVERED PAINTER TOSS WOOLLASTON once suggested that someone who had forged his works would have had his painting hand cut off if he had lived in ancient times. Woollaston knew his history, if not quite the full story: a Roman slave who was caught forging would be sentenced to death.

There have been three known instances of Woollaston's work being forged. In this instance the artist was referring to the travesty that had come to his attention in the mid 1990s and continues to the present day. Rossano Fan, the perpetrator, was born in China, the son of an architect, and moved to New Zealand from Hong Kong in 1963. He was also known as Laocino Ming-Ching Fan and Ming-Ching Fan. Brilliant, gregarious and obsessed with architecture, he worked briefly for an architect in the city of Palmerston North before branching out on his own and establishing a successful modernist practice.

In the early 1970s Fan designed a family home for Toss Woollaston at Riwaka, a small town in the north of the South Island. Although he was a successful architect, Fan appears to have been a frustrated artist. Peter McLeavey, Toss Woollaston's Wellington art dealer, would observe that Fan became enamoured, even obsessed, with the artist's work.

Woollaston regarded and trusted Fan as a friend but this would change when, two decades later, Fan began to forge Woollaston's works. He employed two methods. He overpainted several drawings by Woollaston that he owned with watercolour and sold them as 'collaborations' even though Woollaston had never collaborated with him. And he made complete forgeries from scratch.

In 1996, when he was eighty-six, Woollaston saw some of these forgeries – both overpainted drawings, which he referred to as 'partly faked', and outright forgeries – on sale in an Auckland dealer gallery. He lodged a complaint with the police and the story became a cause célèbre. Fan was quoted in *The New Zealand Herald* as saying in his defence that all apprentices sought enlightenment from the greater masters. 'I'm not a bum you know,' he added. McLeavey felt Fan may have been misguidedly trying to pay homage to his onetime client.

Woollaston thought the forgeries were poor, noting that they differed greatly from his own in colour and composition. In 2014 his son, Philip Woollaston, told me in an interview that the signature Fan had forged was only passable and the works themselves failed on two counts. First, the paper size was wrong, being larger than any of the standard sizes used by his father. Secondly, Fan's palette was too vivid. Woollaston's palette of muddy ochre tones and dull greens was utterly distinctive, as was his expressive style and application of paint, whether watercolour or oil. More representational paintings, such as those of Goldie, might look more complex but in reality they are easier to mimic than Toss Woollaston's sweeping and visible brushstrokes.

Intent on copying Woollaston's work, Fan didn't just tinker with a few examples. More forgeries would soon come to light not only in Auckland but in Wellington and Palmerston North. In January 1997 Woollaston's Auckland dealer, Kerry Aberhart, reported having seen eighteen such works. He wrote to Fan asking him to stop his activities. Fan's reply was to offer Aberhart a commission on any sales he made.

Keen to find out whether forged Woollastons were still being offered for sale twenty years after the artist first saw them in the Auckland gallery, I approached the Peter McLeavey Gallery. I discovered that in 2013 and 2014 at least two collectors had approached the gallery with Woollaston works that turned out to be forgeries. Looking to have the works authenticated with a view to selling them, the owners had been shocked to find they had purchased the work of Fan.

The gallery has a protocol for authenticating Woollaston works. The staff not only scrutinise the paper type and palette but also the information supplied about the painting's subject. Woollaston was meticulous about providing data such as the location, title and date of a painting. Genuine Woollaston works contain all of this; the forged works do not.

Art dealers and auction houses are understandably nervous about inauthentic works: if they sell such a work they can be liable to refund the buyer. Mossgreen-Webb's, a prominent Auckland auction house, includes in its terms and conditions for vendors:

> Fakes, Forgeries, Faults and False Documentation.
> If the purchaser of any lot returns it to Mossgreen-Webb's in the same condition as it was at the time of purchase within the period of 24 months from the date of purchase and believes that it is a fake or a deliberate forgery or was misrepresented within the period of 12 months and it is proved to have had a deliberately disguised or undisclosed repair or that any supporting documentation provided at the time of sale was false or significantly in error as to fact, whether or not the status of the lot was known to the Vendor, the Vendor shall accept the return of the lot and shall refund any money received from Mossgreen-Webb's in respect of that lot. The Vendor agrees to indemnify Mossgreen-Webb's for all reasonable costs endured by Mossgreen-Webb's in justifying a representation made for an item, whether that justification is successful or not.

A provision like this puts the onus squarely on the seller of a work, and offers some comfort to a buyer that they will receive a refund if they find out within the stipulated time frame that a work is a fake or forgery, or has been altered.

However, artists who are the victims of forgers can expect little redress. When Tim Wilson interviewed the detective assigned to the Woollaston case, she told him, 'It's terrible for those involved ... but I've thirty assault files to look at before I get to this.' In 1996 Jane Evans, a Nelson artist, reported that at least three watercolours purportedly signed by her and sold were not her work. Although she made a formal complaint to the police, the case was dropped. The police told her that unless a forger was caught in the act of making the works there was not enough evidence to lay a charge. Evans' word that the works were not by her was not enough.

IN HIS ARTICLE, 'Crook Art', in the *New Zealand Listener* in January 1997, Wilson made the point that the small size of New Zealand's art market meant if there were a sudden bulge in paintings by an artist such as Woollaston someone was likely to notice and wonder why aloud.[12] A bulge in an art market may be legitimate – the result, for example, of an artist's estate releasing works to sell. Reputable auction houses make a feature of such sales, producing glossy catalogues profiling the artist and the origins of the collection. But, as was the case with the rash of Woollaston works, it may result from illegal activity.

In 1999 Trade Me, an online auction site modelled on the American site eBay, was launched in New Zealand and quickly became a popular selling portal for art. Items often sell quickly and with little or no documentation. If a potential buyer starts asking a seller difficult questions about authenticity, the seller may simply remove the item from sale.

In February 2014 four Woollaston works were offered for sale on Trade Me. One had this description:

> This is one of several signed Toss Woollaston works purchased from the family of his artist/architect Rossano Fan. Fan and Woolaston [sic] travelled and painted together in and around the Nelson area. These works are therefore regarded as a collaboration, however the status may well change as further information is gathered on the relationship between the two artists. Although the Woollaston signature is certainly genuine the full extent of the collaboration is unknown. A letter of providence [sic] is provided with the painting.

The wording of the advertisement was quite clever. Describing the signature is 'certainly genuine' subtly suggests an element of doubt about the work. The words 'the status may well change' also provide an out for the seller. Woollaston clearly stated he had never collaborated with Fan. The artist and architect may have travelled and painted together, but they did not paint on the same piece of paper.

With another Trade Me sale offer, a letter of 'provenance' accompanying the work noted it was one of several signed Woollaston works purchased in September 2012 from the family of Rossano Fan. Fan died in July 2014 but his works continue to resurface.

The Toss Woollaston Trust keeps a close eye out for forged works and is happy to assist would-be buyers with questions of provenance and authenticity: on some occasions they have issued certificates of authenticity. The trustees clearly do not want to see the reputation and legacy of one of New Zealand's greatest artists, honoured with a knighthood for his services to art, compromised in any way.

Not all Woollaston frauds involve Rossano Fan. Three paintings that bear no signature and no resemblance to Woollaston's work have been offered at least twice to dealers as 'early Woollastons', with a story that the purchaser of the artist's Riwaka house in the early 1990s was given them by the artist. In each case a dealer approached Philip Woollaston seeking to authenticate the paintings. They were clearly not by the artist. Philip Woollaston thinks these works by other artists may have been in the possession of one or other of his parents, and have been discarded or inadvertently left behind when his father moved house in 1992.

Colin McCahon withdrawn

THERE IS ALWAYS A LEVEL OF EXCITEMENT when a work by New Zealand's foremost modernist painter comes up for auction. There are only so many McCahons out there and they often reach record-breaking prices.

In July 2014 *Elias*, painted in 1959, looked to be a welcome addition to the auction scene. The work had spent much of its existence in the collection of Doris Lusk, a fellow painter, friend and contemporary of Colin McCahon. A photograph taken by Marti Friedlander in 1978 showed Lusk with part of her outstanding art collection. *Elias* was hanging alongside other works by McCahon and paintings by Rita Angus and Trevor Moffitt.

Elias was listed in Webb's auction house's glossy catalogue as 660 x 430 mm with an estimated price of $250,000 to $300,000. Its materials were described as 'enamel on board', a rather simplistic description: potential buyers of such a painting should be given comprehensive details of the materials and methods McCahon used. In Friedlander's photograph *Elias* appeared to have an uneven surface. This could have resulted from the addition of materials such as sand or sawdust to the paint, a common practice of McCahon's at the time.

Peter Simpson, the author of the essay about McCahon in the catalogue, noted: 'Of the thirteen *Elias* paintings, all but two are painted with enamel housepaints (Solpah and Butex) on hard-board.'[13] However, he did not say if the *Elias* painting in the Webb's auction was one of the two exceptions.

The key to the condition of McCahon works is usually related to the artist's experimentation with paints and surfaces. In New Zealand, a country with a high proportion of weatherboard houses, we know that commercial paints can have a limited life. During the period when McCahon was painting, weatherboard homes were usually repainted every five or so years. Obviously works made with commercial paints can have a long and stable existence if they are housed in a climate-controlled environment, as may be the case in a public art gallery, although even then there will inevitably be some deterioration. They don't fare as well in a domestic situation, where levels of temperature and humidity will fluctuate.

In 1958 Colin McCahon spent four months visiting the United States, where he witnessed the work of contemporaries such as Jackson Pollock. World-renowned for his drip paintings, Pollock had devised a method of applying paint that flouted Western art traditions. He used industrial and household paints, pouring and splattering them on to his canvases with great physical gusto and creating myriad free-formed lines.

What McCahon saw in America spurred him to approach his own practice afresh. As Pollock had found, household enamel paints flowed well. For McCahon, who liked to include text in his compositions, this was an added bonus on top of the obvious financial savings.

He was not alone in experimenting with paint at this time. Other artists such as Ted Bracey were trying adding PVA and then overvarnishing, the end result being a long slow yellowing of the entire work that would provide to be beyond remedial conservation. (In the 1990s another artist, Peter Robinson, would deliberately use paints that changed over time, resulting in works with a possibly limited life span. The addition of bitumen, the material used to construct roads, meant slow erosion in the surfaces. This was intended to symbolise the erosion of Māori culture.)

In her 2000 book *Beneath the Surface*, co-written with Kendrah Morgan, art curator and conservator Sarah Hillary described McCahon's newfound artistic freedom as the work of 'an intentional nonconformist, an anti-academic painter'. For decades, partly due to a lack of art supplies during the war years, artists in Western Europe and America had experimented with non-traditional materials. They had also abandoned perfectly prepared canvases, preferring to paint on unstretched ones. Taking a lead from this, McCahon began to paint on doors, which could be exhibited without any kind of framing.

In 1959 he embarked on the *Elias* series. He would later suggest he had made approximately a hundred works in the series, but neither the original *Elias* exhibition list nor the *Colin McCahon Online Catalogue* gives any indication of there being more than fifteen or sixteen paintings that can be considered part of the series.

PEOPLE ATTENDING WEBB'S JULY AUCTION were stunned when at the last minute the very desirable *Elias* painting was withdrawn. A quarterly auction round-up in *Art News New Zealand* later noted that the painting's removal had caused palpable disappointment in the room. No explanation was given.

On August 3 *The Sunday Star-Times* reported it had obtained a condition report on the painting via an automatic request button on Webb's website. This report, which had been available prior to the auction, stated the work had 'undergone some restorative treatment' and that retouching had been applied 'where movement/craquelure has resulted in slight but visually discernible breaks in the imagery'. In keeping with good conservation practice, all treatment that had been applied was removable, the report stated. The work itself was 'sound and stable' and would 'no doubt be remembered as one of the finest paintings by Colin McCahon presented at auction'.

It all read convincingly enough. Webb's had offered an account of the treatment the painting had undergone and described its current condition. That remedial work had been carried out was not untoward: dealers and auction houses can and do suggest this if they deem it necessary. Webb's own terms and conditions of sale clearly stated:

> Webb's reserves the right to have any remedial work done to the goods at the Vendor's cost if in its opinion such is required to make the goods more saleable.

However, the reputation of the painting had now changed irrevocably. Although the work had exceptional provenance, the amount of treatment it had received and the publicity this had gained in the media had cast a shadow.

Christopher Swasbrook, the chair of Webb's, told *The Sunday Star-Times* that 'restoration of such pieces is common and is required to ensure that they are available to be viewed and enjoyed in the future'. But the question was how much conservation or restoration work is too much? And if a work has had a large amount of restorative treatment, does it lose value and become in effect a second-rate painting?

Conservation and restoration are different, and the terms are not interchangeable. Conservation, which is supported and practised by public art galleries, involves stabilising a work and preventing it from further deterioration. Restoration is about retouching and repainting areas to make a painting look as it did when first created, and this can have detrimental effects.

Sophie Coupland, the head of Webb's fine art department, defended the price estimate of $250,000 to $300,000 the company had put on the work, telling *Sunday Star-Times* reporter Kim Knight they had taken into consideration its condition, which was far from original. 'We knew it had condition issues, there was no two ways about that,' she was reported as saying. *He Calls for Elias*, a work from the same series, had sold at auction in 2011 for $562,500. However, that work had been slightly larger than Webb's *Elias* – the size of a painting can have an effect on its value – and was in a better state.

In 2016 I contacted Webb's (by then Mossgreen-Webb's) for further information about this case. I wanted to know what events had led to Webb's withdrawal of the painting. Had the seller demanded it be withdrawn because of the remedial work that had been done on it, or had Webb's themselves made this decision?

My questions were essentially:

- Would it be possible to have a copy of the condition report? Although there had originally been one online it was no longer there when I looked.
- The company had been very transparent about *Elias*, saying it had had work done to it and that the estimate price reflected this. So, what made them withdraw it – and how did the media get on to the story so quickly?
- Works don't often get withdrawn from auction, and when they do the public will jump to the conclusion it's because of questions of provenance/ownership or the work's condition. Was this a case of being nervous around the remedial work and deciding to withdraw the painting without considering the wider ramifications for it, the auction

> house, and the individuals involved? Or was it the vendor who withdrew it?

I received no reply. I later learned that another auction house had been offered the work but decided it wasn't in a good enough condition to sell.

ALTHOUGH *ELIAS* WAS WITHDRAWN FROM AUCTION and returned to the vendor, the case demonstrates that any potential buyer of an artwork should ask probing questions until fully satisfied with the answers given and the evidence provided. Everything may not be what it seems. Once the gavel falls any redress may be long and expensive. And, as is the way with a leaky house, once a painting has been called into question it may lose its market appeal. In some eyes this *Elias* will be forever tainted.

FIVE

The loss of Psyche

WHEN THE ROBERT MCDOUGALL ART GALLERY in Christchurch's Botanic Gardens opened in 1932 it housed a permanent collection of 160 works. A small team of staff took care of the collection and its purpose-built gallery. For the first sixteen years, until the gallery began to host touring exhibitions, the collection remained static and regular visitors got to know the works well, often referring to them simply by their catalogue number.[14]

In 1942, and again during the 1950s or '60s, paintings disappeared under mysterious circumstances. *Psyche*, a 1902 work by a British artist, Solomon Joseph Solomon, vanished on the night of June 21, 1942 or in the early hours of the following day. Solomon was a versatile painter whose work had ranged from formal portraits, mainly done to earn a living, to dramatic scenes from mythology. In the missing painting, Psyche, the goddess of love, lies unashamedly naked and resplendent.

Given the erotic nature of the work, it was thought the theft of the almost life-size female nude – the painting measured 900 x 1530 mm – was probably a male prank. American servicemen who, when they were on leave, sometimes caught the ferry to Christchurch for the weekend, came under suspicion. As they were fit and agile, perhaps one of them had scaled the walls and entered the gallery via the roof? A later curator at the gallery, Neil Roberts, would speculate: 'I can't see New Zealanders particularly liking that painting then. It would have fitted the American "pin-up" kind of culture.' But while this version of events makes for good reading and has become cemented in the gallery's history, there is no evidence to support it.

It is known that when the gallery's custodian, Horace Palmer, arrived on the morning of June 22 he found *Psyche* missing from its place in the Centre South Gallery. The thief or thieves had removed the canvas from its frame for ease of handling and left behind both the frame and the stretcher, suggesting those responsible had not left the building by a normal method, such as through a door. Palmer also found wax matches strewn over the floor.

Next day the local newspaper, *The Press*, reported that piecing the puzzle together was proving difficult. An examination of the building had revealed that four windows bore signs of having been tampered with. Panes were broken in a window at the back of the building, and in a window on the roof to which access could have been gained via an overhanging tree. Another window in the roof had a damaged catch, and a window in the front of the building had been opened and left ajar.[15]

Although the gallery was of a classical architectural design, it had some modern features, including a series of skylights that filtered natural light into each room of the gallery, with the exception of the print room, which was kept in subdued light to protect its works on paper. It was assumed that the culprits had entered through one of these skylights. The architect, Edward Armstrong, had designed innovative blinds fixed behind all the skylights. These could be pulled down on bright days to keep light levels constant and protect the art from unnecessary damage. However, doing so was apparently a rigmarole and the blinds were rarely adjusted.

As architectural drawings for the building showed, the roof layout was complex, therefore anyone planning on breaking and entering needed to have intimate knowledge of the design. Significantly, the skylights were not part of the exterior roof: there was an enclosed area between them and the roof. This space, approximately five by six metres, had enough headroom to enable a person to stand up in it. You could enter it from the roof by lifting up a window. To then open a skylight and drop the considerable distance to the gallery floor would, however, be a dangerous undertaking.

IN 2014 I VISITED THE CRIME SCENE to try to figure out how the painting had been spirited out of the building. I wasn't the first to have attempted this in recent times. In June 2002, after seventy years as the city's main repository of public art, the McDougall Art Gallery had closed and the following year the collection had moved to the newly built Christchurch Art Gallery Te Puna o Waiwhetu. The disappearance of *Psyche* had puzzled Neil Roberts since he joined the McDougall in 1979. As staff prepared to leave the building he decided to explore the roof area to see if it held any clues. He soon realised it was impossible to enter the gallery from the rooftop: the catches for the skylight windows were inside the gallery.

The McDougall was empty when I visited, making it easy to spend an afternoon clambering over the roof, trying to reenact the events of June 1942. Like Roberts, I established that, unless some preparation had been carried out ahead of time, the thief or thieves could not have entered the Centre South Gallery, where the painting hung, via the roof: the catch for the skylight could not be opened from the rooftop cavity. In fact the window above the Centre South Gallery seemed to be in its original condition and showed no sign of ever having been forced open or repaired, contrary to reports in *The Press* immediately after the theft. Breaking into the roof cavity would have been even more difficult as the glass was reinforced.

Even if the thief or thieves had managed to get in – if, say, the skylight had been deliberately left open for them – it was at least a four-metre drop to the floor. To make it safely the thief would have to have had a rope or ladder left in position under the skylight – and this is on the assumption they had managed to get on to the roof in the first place. In 1942 there were no adjacent buildings and the nearest large trees were not close enough to allow a person to jump from one of them on to the roof. The gallery's exterior walls were flush and approximately eight metres tall, making them difficult to scale, especially by a person carrying heavy tools such as a crowbar.

There was another impediment for a would-be thief. The surface of the roof, not visible from ground level, was made up of numerous caps, which lay beyond the building's parapet. These caps were on several different levels and could be accessed only by using ladders. Without a torch – and the matches strewn on the gallery floor likely indicated the thief did not have one – it would have been tricky to navigate the roof without prior knowledge.

And if by a miracle the burglars had got into the gallery, ripped *Psyche* out of its frame, and escaped out of one of the front windows, they would have had trouble leaving the Botanic Gardens. Each night the gardens were locked at dusk. The bridges that straddled the adjacent Avon River had a row of spikes to deter people climbing in and out of the gardens. And given it was raining that night, the whole episode began to seem increasingly mysterious.

AN INTERESTING QUESTION is why anyone would have gone to such trouble to steal the painting. It was wartime and interest in investing in Victorian paintings was at an all-time low, so we can speculate with some certainty that *Psyche* wasn't stolen to order. There was no market for such works in New Zealand, and transporting a painting offshore – even without a frame – would not have been easy.

Although the theft was reported in *The Press*, the incident was treated in a low-key manner: there seems to have been little official interest or ongoing police investigation: the police file contains only the stories from the newspaper. Even more curiously, the custodian, Horace Palmer, who was responsible for security at the gallery, did not mention the theft in his daily report to the city council, nor in his annual report at the end of the year.

FOUR DECADES LATER, out of the blue, hopes were raised for the painting's recovery. Nineteen eighty-two was the fiftieth anniversary of the opening of the gallery. After a feature article about the gallery in which *Psyche*'s disappearance was mentioned appeared in *The Press*, an Ashburton man came forward. He recalled seeing the painting in a Napier home. A call was put out in Napier's evening newspaper *Hawke's Bay Today* and soon afterwards a man phoned to say he had a painting of a life-size reclining nude that could be confused with *Psyche*. His brother had painted it while at art school in Christchurch. The Napier house fitted the description given by the Ashburton man.

Later that year the gallery anonymously received a Polaroid photograph of what was at first believed to be *Psyche*. Because the envelope had a Christchurch postmark there was hope the painting was not far from the gallery and in good condition. Soon afterwards *The Press* reported that the photograph had been a hoax. The prankster had made a copy of the work, guessing at the painting's palette as only black and white images of the original were available, and then taken the Polaroid. In a piece of doggerel, he had confessed:

> Dear Sir,
> Psyches sleep, Psyches awake
> Some are real, some are fake
> Masterpieces are seldom met,
> Touch this one, the paint is still wet.

Today, nearly seventy-five years after *Psyche* disappeared, the chance of finding it appears slim. All that remains is the impressive tabernacle-style gilt-finished frame in storage at Christchurch Art Gallery. Naked frames like this are a reminder to the public of the fragility and vulnerability of art collections. Public galleries and museums that have been robbed of a work sometimes continue to hang the empty frame to educate audiences about the loss and possibly jog some memories. Perhaps the best example is Boston's Isabella Stewart Gardner Museum. The empty frames of the museum's thirteen stolen works still grace the walls.

SOMETIME AFTER THE LOSS OF *PSYCHE*, a second painting vanished from the McDougall. *Leda and the Swan*, painted around 1868 by French artist Adolphe Jourdan, had been gifted to the gallery in 1932 by Canterbury College of the University of New Zealand. A large erotic work, it depicted the mythological story in which Zeus, the king of the gods, in the form of a swan rapes Leda as she sleeps with her husband, King Tyndareus. This has been a favourite subject of many artists, from Michelangelo and Leonardo da Vinci to Paul Cézanne, and of poets such as W.B. Yeats. The painting had been first exhibited soon after its creation as *Jupiter and Leda* at London's Victoria and Albert Museum, Jupiter being the Roman equivalent of the Greek god Zeus.

Both Solomon's *Psyche* and Jourdan's *Leda and the Swan* were striking examples of Academicism, a style that had its roots in nineteenth-century French art, particularly that of the Académie des Beaux-Arts. These highly polished and detailed works usually depicted a mythological or historical subject. *Leda and the Swan*, when exhibited at Melbourne's International Exhibition of 1880 to 1881, was described as 'an academical study' and the profile of Leda as 'exceedingly beautiful'. When *Psyche* was exhibited at the New Zealand International Exhibition in Christchurch's Hagley Park in 1906 and 1907, the official publication described it as 'an outstanding example of a beautiful pose, accurate drawing, and perfection of flesh tones', and noted that it had originally been purchased by the Canterbury Society of Arts for £440.

Leda and the Swan presided over the McDougall's South Gallery. Not everyone was fond of it. When George Bernard Shaw visited the McDougall in 1934, he was asked what he thought of the collection. He suggested *Leda and the Swan* should be kept on permanent display as an example to students of how not to paint.

In May 1949 the South Gallery was emptied in order to accommodate a loan exhibition, *Contemporary British Prints and Drawings selected from the Wakefield Collection*, which had come to New Zealand courtesy of the British Council. It is likely that the works removed from the gallery were stored in the building's basement but it is not clear if *Leda and the Swan* was among them: in 1948, when a part-time honorary curator, William Baverstock, joined the gallery, he had made a complete inventory of the entire collection and *Leda and the Swan* was not on the list.

The only clear image of the painting known to be in existence was in a small oil painting of the gallery's interior, which had been produced by an artist, John Knight, in 1935. The work could also be seen distantly in a photograph of the exhibition hall at an 1882 New Zealand international exhibition in Christchurch. (More recently Neil Roberts made a serendipitous find on the US auction site eBay of an etching of *Leda and the Swan*; this is now a valuable visual resource in the gallery's files.)

In the late 1970s Roberts, newly employed by the McDougall, had searched for *Leda and the Swan* and found it missing. The painting's large size, 2050 x 1500 mm, its ornate frame and considerable weight meant it could not have been removed without a great deal of effort. The basement, where it was supposedly stored after the evacuation of the South Gallery, housed among other things the custodian's cleaning equipment and tools. When Horace Palmer was questioned, the only light he could shed on the situation was that *Leda and the Swan* had got in the way of his buckets. In November 1944 the painting was one of five that had been damaged while hanging in the gallery. Truant schoolboys were thought to be responsible although this was never proved. Could the fact *Leda and the Swan* was damaged have led Palmer to think it could be disposed of?

There were other possibilities. Both *Psyche* and *Leda and the Swan* depicted female nudes. Could someone have taken offence at the subject matter and deliberately removed the paintings and disposed of them? If so the works would not have been the first in the history of art to suffer such a fate. When the great English Romantic painter J.M.W. Turner died in 1851, the thousands of works he left behind included, as well as his famous landscape paintings, several explicit drawings of prostitutes. John Ruskin, the executor of Turner's estate, instructed staff at London's National Gallery to burn the drawings so Turner's reputation would not be sullied, and this was carried out in 1858.

Closer to home, when Whanganui artist Edith Collier returned to her family home to live in her early thirties, after years studying in England with painters such as Frances Hodgkins, her father threw all her works depicting female nudes on to a bonfire, ruining years of work and blighting a promising career.

As recently as 2012 London metropolitan police removed an artwork that was on exhibition at a dealer gallery, claiming it condoned bestiality. The lenticular photograph by Derrick Santini, *A Fool for Love*, was a modern take on the story of Leda and the swan. It seems this Greek myth can still cause ructions in the art world.

COULD BOTH *PSYCHE* AND *LEDA AND THE SWAN* have been victims of inside jobs? Among numerous theories put forward over the years is that a cleaner damaged *Psyche* and, in an effort to cover it up, staged a phony burglary. This is feasible: crimes committed by gallery staff are not unknown. Between 1995 and 2002, for example, Keith Davies, an employee of New Zealand's National Army Museum, stole 843 medals worth about $256,000 from the museum's collection. When the crime was discovered in 2011 Davies returned from Australia, pleaded guilty, and was convicted and sentenced to three years' imprisonment. Only 300 of the medals were recovered. This was the second embarrassment for the army museum. In December 2007, ninety-six war medals had been taken in a smash and grab. After extensive publicity the two men responsible had been found, convicted and sent to jail.

Another inside job concerned a portrait of Winston Churchill. Graham Sutherland, a fifty-year-old modernist artist, had been commissioned by members of the House of Commons and House of Lords to paint the portrait in 1954 to celebrate the former British prime minister's eightieth birthday. Both Churchill and his wife Clementine hated the picture from the moment they saw it. At the unveiling ceremony, which took place in front of a large audience and was filmed by the BBC, Churchill described it ambiguously as a 'remarkable example of modern art'.

For years the couple stored the painting in the basement of their home and skirted around questions as to what had happened to it. It was not until 2015, with the publication of a biography, *First Lady: The Life and Wars of Clementine Churchill*, that the truth emerged. After Churchill's death his wife had asked the couple's long-serving secretary Grace Hamblin to dispose of the work. With the help of her brother, Hamblin had removed it at night from Chartwell and thrown it on a bonfire at her brother's property.

ALTHOUGH MANY DISAPPEARANCES of artworks are never solved, some works do find their way back home. On January 6, 1985 a third painting was stolen from the McDougall Art Gallery. Dated 1883, *The Fountain* by William Breakspeare, a painter based in Birmingham, depicted a woman leaning over the edge of fountain. The painting's small size, 220 x 315 mm, made it an easy target for thieves. The gallery had hung it as part of a massive 600-work exhibition called *Artfull*, which it had undertaken in the process of reorganising its storage. The exhibition would, in the gallery's words, 'allow Christchurch to see works which had not been shown for many years'.

On January 31, 1985 Christchurch police returned the painting to the gallery. The work was still intact and the gallery's staff were told not to ask any questions. They were intrigued to discover it had gained a splattering of what appeared to be tomato sauce.

THERE IS AN INTERESTING POSTSCRIPT to the stories of *Psyche* and *Leda and the Swan*. In recent years works by both Solomon Joseph Solomon and Adolphe Jourdan, long out of fashion, have begun to enjoy a renaissance. In 2009 *The Birth of Eve*, painted by Solomon in 1908, hit the headlines when it sold at Christie's auction house in London for £713, 250 to a private collector in Australia. A much larger work than *Psyche*, it too depicted a female nude. The painting had been de-accessioned from the collection of London's Ealing Council on the grounds that it did not meet the collection's criteria and was also too large for the council to exhibit safely. An 1889 work by Jourdan, *Tendresse Maternelle*, much smaller than *Leda and the Swan* at 900 x 700 mm, sold in Paris in November 2014 for €13,000.

FIVE

Urewera Mural

AT FOUR O'CLOCK ON THE MORNING of June 5, 1997 a security alarm pierced the air at Lake Waikaremoana, an isolated spot in the heart of New Zealand's Te Urewera National Park. Glenn Mitchell, the area chief for the Department of Conservation, which managed the national park, heard it from his home and quickly made his way to the park's visitor centre. A large floor-to-ceiling window was broken. Inside the building it was quickly evident that all three panels of the park's iconic *Urewera Mural* by painter Colin McCahon had disappeared.

In 1975 McCahon had been commissioned by the Urewera Park Trust Board to execute a large work for the park's new visitor centre. The theme was to be 'the mystery of man in the Urewera'. McCahon was an obvious choice for the commission. Today considered one of New Zealand's foremost artists, he was already well established as a modernist, with a devout love and understanding of the land.

McCahon proceeded with great endeavour to produce a work that reflected the history of the local Tūhoe people and their land.

The respected Māori curator and art historian Jonathan Mane-Wheoki would later say the painting was made at the cusp of change. The year it was commissioned the Treaty of Waitangi Act was passed, giving legal status to the Crown's 1840 treaty with Māori for the first time, and setting up a body, the Waitangi Tribunal, to hear claims over title to land and other assets. At this time, too, New Zealand artists were increasingly attuned to the international art scene through seeing touring exhibitions and travelling abroad. Artists such as McCahon were changing the course of New Zealand art: he himself would become one of the first New Zealand painters to be recognised overseas.

A deeply spiritual person, McCahon chose to compose the painting as a triptych. Like triptychs that are found at the altars of cathedrals, *Urewera Mural* references Christianity: the play on the number three is synonymous with the Holy Trinity. But unlike its cathedral predecessors, which were often painted on wood panels, *Urewera Mural* was made on unstretched canvases of cotton duck, a form of canvas that differs from the linen variety, which is made from flax. Although the work has been documented as being made with acrylic paint, McCahon seems to have used a mixture of paints. Conservator Sarah Hillary told me her impression was that the paint was not just synthetic polymer emulsion (acrylic and/or PVA) but probably alkyd or oil. The paint of the large T form in the central panel was much thicker and more rigid so unlikely to be acrylic.

McCahon was no stranger to working on a large format and the finished size of *Urewera Mural*, which he painted in his studio at Muriwai Beach near Auckland, was 2550 x 5445 mm. The triptych arrangement allowed him to explore his favourite themes of life and death, as well as paying homage to gods from both Māori and European belief systems. Multi-layered and rich in symbolism and meaning, the work depicted aspects of Tūhoe history and mythology, and referenced Te Kooti, the guerilla fighter and founder of the Ringatū religion, and the Tūhoe prophet Rua Kēnana. The large T could have a number of meanings: a waterfall; the trunk of a totara tree; T for Tūhoe, or Tane, the guardian of the forest, or Theos, Greek for god; or a modernist cruciform. The right-hand branch of the T contained a star from the flag of rebel leader Te Kooti.

The work also included text, which had by then become a familiar motif of McCahon's work. Jonathan Mane-Wheoki noted that Māori who viewed the painting were comfortable with the inclusion of words as these had historically been attached to taonga, or treasures, as a way of conveying stories and messages. Words also cause viewers to linger as they contemplate their meaning. In this sense *Urewera Mural* could be seen as an altarpiece: meditation through reading was part of its engagement.

From the outset, part of the painting's appeal was speculation about the meaning behind every word and form. McCahon had told his dealer Peter McLeavey: 'Tane in the middle, the Tuhoe People on the left & Rua & Te Kooti on the right – and the Tuhoe who continue.' The right-hand panel contained the words 'Tuhoe', 'Urewera' and 'Their Land'. Members of the Park Board were anxious, and asked several times for revisions. Asking an artist to make changes to a work that has been carefully researched and is already underway is not an insignificant step. Indeed, McCahon may have felt insulted because in January 1976 he wrote a letter withdrawing from the commission. However, he didn't post it and instead pressed ahead making the changes requested.

Interestingly McCahon may have had the final say, as the original words can be read under the finished text. In one area it looks as though the earlier text has been literally scrubbed off the surface. He signed and dated the painting 'March–July 1975'. It was hung at eye level in the visitor centre's Māori hall by the building's architect, John Scott, and unveiled the following year.

Two years later, in a special edition of the journal *Art New Zealand* dedicated to McCahon's work, art critic Neil Rowe wrote of *Urewera Mural*: 'In this smouldering beautiful painting McCahon depicts the brooding majesty of the Urewera country, and also the inseparable bond between the people and the land which is the very essence of Māoritanga and which should be the heritage of all New Zealanders.'

With funding from a local family trust and the Queen Elizabeth II Arts Council, McCahon had been paid $4,000 for the work. When it was stolen it was valued at $1.2 million.

GLENN MITCHELL HAD SEEN a Toyota Corolla speeding away from the crime scene. Department of Conservation workers quickly set up a road block. Later they would discover they had unknowingly stopped the perpetrators, who had transferred the artwork from the Toyota Corolla to the back of a blue Bedford van and hidden it under a mattress in the back. The Corolla was found burnt out at a dump in the small town of Ruatāhuna thirty-two kilometres away.

The heist of *Urewera Mural* created a media storm. Although the work was in a remote location and few New Zealanders had seen it, McCahon was an established artist with a big reputation and the public was shocked and angered. The art world was particularly devastated. Many worried about the condition of the work, knowing it could easily and rapidly deteriorate if not cared for properly. It had obviously been taken at great speed and more than likely rolled up and flung into the getaway car, a sedan with a boot.

Early on the police suspected the theft was politically motivated but it was two weeks before an investigative team was set up. Dubbed 'Operation Art', it was led by Inspector Graham Bell. Tame Iti, a well-known Tūhoe activist, came under immediate suspicion. Interviewed on June 5, he claimed the first he knew of the painting's disappearance was when he received a telephone call from another Tūhoe activist, Te Kaha. The following day, television channel TV3 contacted Tame Iti and informed him the police were on their way to his house. Thirty-five officers searched his property and failed to find the mural. Iti was arrested for possession of firearms, assault and kidnapping. He claimed to have been sorting out some local 'hoods' who had been carrying out home invasions, hence the weapons.

Other Tūhoe were not keen to speak to the police and in a short space of time the situation became very tense. Pressure on the police mounted as the nation became increasingly upset about the loss of a national treasure. An Auckland lawyer, Christopher Harder, decided a go-between was needed to meet with Te Kaha and Tame Iti, diffuse the situation and secure the painting's return. One candidate was Jenny Gibbs, an avid art collector, philanthropist, and member of the board of Te Papa. Gibbs was a connoisseur of McCahon's work and thought to have the right mix of quiet diplomacy and a genuine interest in the artist.

Gibbs agreed to assist, but one of her early conditions was that Harder back away and leave her to carry out the task. Another condition was that no ransom was to be paid for the painting's return, or for information about its whereabouts. She would do everything within her powers but under no circumstances would she or any other agency be 'buying back' *Urewera Mural.*

Over several months, trust and understanding developed among Tame Iti, Te Kaha and Jenny Gibbs. She was alarmed to learn that the mural had been buried in the ground, and gave the men packing materials, including plastic bubble wrap, to try and prevent it being damaged by dampness. She also spent much time educating them about McCahon and the three visited Auckland Art Gallery to view his work. Gibbs wanted them to understand the significance of McCahon's art and his strong empathy with Tūhoe and their deep affiliation with their land.

Tame Iti and Te Kaha now had a dilemma. As the artwork was so well known they couldn't sell it: no dealer or collector would touch it. And it had already served its purpose of drawing attention to Tūhoe grievances. At one stage they threatened to cut it up to show what it was like to have something precious damaged, but fortunately thought better of the idea.

The anticipated return of *Urewera Mural* was on-again off-again. When Tame Iti and Te Kaha requested a helicopter, Gibbs organised for one owned by her former husband, Alan Gibbs, to be on standby with a pilot. Then on August 29, 1998, she received a telephone call from Te Kaha. He was driving to Auckland from Ruatāhuna. The mural was in his car. Gibbs was to meet him on a street in the suburb of One Tree Hill.

Gibbs drove her Mitsubishi station wagon to the rendezvous. Not wanting to be charged with being in possession of stolen goods should the painting be handed to her, she had taken the precaution of having the Department of Conservation, the legal owners of *Urewera Mural*, nominate her as their agent.

At the meeting spot she was blindfolded and Te Kaha took over driving her car. The pair arrived at an unknown destination, where they collected the painting. Te Kaha then drove a short distance before allowing Gibbs to remove the blindfold and take over driving. She and Te Kaha went directly to the Auckland Art Gallery, where Sarah Hillary met them and took possession of the painting. Immediately after this, Gibbs notified the police that the painting had been returned.

Although securing the return of such a valuable painting had been a serious undertaking, it had had its funny moments. Gibbs reported that when the police came to her home in exclusive Paratai Drive that evening to take her statement, they asked if she knew of Te Kaha's current whereabouts. 'Oh yes,' she replied, 'he's upstairs asleep. It was a long night of driving for him.' It was not quite the answer they had expected.

The police were critical of the liaison, seeing Gibbs as simply getting in the way of their operation. However, neither Tame Iti nor Te Kaha trusted the police, and without Gibbs' intervention the mural may never have been returned. Jenny Gibbs was afterwards made an honorary Tūhoe and enjoys an ongoing friendship with Te Kaha, whose work as a carver she greatly admires.

UREWERA MURAL WAS NOT in great shape. The large work had been stored under much less than ideal conditions, and to get it into vehicles it had been folded and rolled up. The painted surface was badly abraded through having been rubbed or scraped. Sarah Hillary, who worked on it after its return, also noted there was dirt and mould, although it was likely the mould had begun while the painting was installed at the visitor centre, induced by the damp Urewera conditions and the lack of climate control in the building.

At his trial Te Kaha pleaded guilty to the theft and received a sentence of 200 hours' community service, to be undertaken at the Auckland Art Gallery. He was also sentenced to fifteen months in prison but this was suspended: although he had previous convictions he had not offended for nine years. Laurie Salmon Davis, an unemployed young man from Ruatoki who had assisted Te Kaha uplift the mural, also pleaded guilty. Te Kaha defended Davis, saying he had not understood the politics behind the act and just 'did it for me'. In reality Davis had a catalogue of previous convictions. He was sent to jail for twelve months. Tame Iti, who had not been involved in the theft, was not charged.

Urewera Mural had been lost for fifteen months. Where had it been during this time? In 2013 Tame Iti divulged that it had finally been left, rolled up like a mat, with a Ruatāhuna weaver, who was said to have had no idea what she was protecting. Fearful of being watched and listened to, Iti and his associates had referred to the painting as 'te whāriki', the floor covering. According to a newspaper report, the weaver was subsequently paid for her time and costs, athough this has not been verified.

MUCH HAS BEEN WRITTEN about this episode under different academic disciplines, including cultural studies and history. But what about art history – was this an art crime? The perpetrators had no intention of selling the painting – the most common motive for art theft – and no one of sound mind would have purchased it anyway, despite the scarcity of McCahon's work on the market. Te Kaha's lawyer, Alan Webb, told the court his client's objective was to protest grievances about the 'removal of the lakes and mountains from the Tūhoe people'. Outside the court, Te Kaha said: 'I have always maintained I did not steal the McCahon. I took it for a while, but I did not steal it.'

The Department of Conservation describes the work as having been stolen, but various other commentators have used terms such as 'spirited away', 'borrowed', 'kidnapped', 'liberated', 'subject to non-consensual removal', and 'an example of cultural activism'. Each term has a different connotation, and some are more loaded than others. Some art crime researchers and writers see this kind of theft as 'terrorist' activity, based on the idea that terrorists have a motive, and will use various means to achieve their goal. In *Art Crime*, John Conklin noted that art theft is well suited to this, being 'calculated to show people that their leaders cannot protect even their culture's most revered objects, thereby suggesting that the leaders are also incapable of serving the citizenry in other ways'. This could be applied to the taking of *Urewera Mural*. Tūhoe demonstrated that a prized painting about their history, land and people by the country's most notable artist was able to be readily removed.

There are international precedents for taking an artwork hostage for political gain. In a well-publicised example from 1961, a disabled old-age pensioner, Kempton Bunton, stole Goya's *Portrait of the Duke of Wellington* from London's National Gallery to protest against pensioners having to pay for television licences. Bunton returned the painting but was convicted of the theft of the frame, which was not returned, and sentenced to three months in prison.

In 1974 nineteen extremely valuable paintings were lifted from a private home in County Wicklow, Dublin. The motive was to use them as bargaining chips to have Irish prisoners serving life sentences transferred from mainland British jails to a jail in Northern Ireland. The perpetrator offered to return five paintings to secure the deal and to return the remaining works in exchange for cash. The attempt failed: all the paintings were recovered in County Cork a few weeks later and the culprit, Rose Dugdale, was sentenced to nine years' imprisonment. She had been accompanied by three members of the IRA.

Colin McCahon was not alive at the time of the heist of *Urewera Mural*: he had died ten years earlier. I asked William McCahon, his son, if he thought the act was an art crime. He said he didn't see it that way, but rather as 'the assertion of mana, and political adventurism'. It is indisputable that because of the incident Tūhoe's plight gained increased public awareness. At a talk in front of *Urewera Mural* at Whakatāne Museum in 2013, Tame Iti was asked if the painting's 'theft' had worked for Tūhoe. He replied that it had worked inasmuch as it created discussion. Tūhoe, he said, had had to do something to make people think.

UREWERA MURAL UNDERWENT around $5,000 of conservation work. It was then exhibited at Auckland Art Gallery and toured to galleries in New Plymouth, Wellington and Whangarei, giving the public the opportunity to view the newsmaking artwork. The question next arose of how to return it safely to the Āniwaniwa Visitor Centre at Waikaremoana and ensure it could not be stolen again. A new gallery space was designed and security measures put in place.

Not everyone was sanguine about the mural's return. Tūhoe felt aggrieved that, for all the publicity, their historic land claims had still not been settled. In September 2000, as government minister

Sandra Lee arrived for the opening ceremony, protesters brandished signs and Te Kaha declared the painting did not 'celebrate the union of Tūhoe people and the New Zealand people'. A skirmish broke out and Tame Iti attacked a Television New Zealand camera with a spear.

Although the painting was now home again, its notoriety had increased its value to two million dollars, making it too expensive to insure. Five years later, Jonathan Mane-Wheoki estimated it was worth three and a half million dollars. Value, though, is a complicated idea. Monetary and artistic values are part of a Western world view. Māori may apply a different set of values, seeing a work such as *Urewera Mural* as a taonga, owned communally and valued not for money or artistry but for its social and cultural importance.

That *Urewera Mural* was made by a Pākehā artist further complicates its value. Ian Wedde, an arts commentator, suggested there was 'tension and even competition' between the artist's signature and Tūhoe sovereignty, but concluded the Western value system had played a part in the incident:

> The most commonly proposed scenario for the heist was the economic value of the painting made it a valuable political hostage, against which such issues as land rights could be negotiated.

In 2011 Mane-Wheoki would describe *Urewera Mural* as New Zealand's most politically charged painting of the twentieth century.

TŪHOE HAD NOT BEEN GIVEN the opportunity to sign the Treaty of Waitangi with the British Crown in 1840, and had seen their best land forcibly confiscated in 1866. Two years later, when the charismatic Poverty Bay leader Te Kooti sought refuge in the Urewera after escaping from exile on the Chatham Islands, the iwi elders pledged to support him as their spiritual leader.

The government sent armed forces in pursuit of Te Kooti and launched a scorched earth policy. Large numbers of Tūhoe were killed. The iwi were finally forced to submit after enduring starvation and countless atrocities. Te Kooti's whereabouts were never revealed, and in 1883 he received an official pardon from the government.

Over the centuries Tūhoe's sense of grievance at their loss of land festered and grew. On October 15, 2007, this was exarcerbated when armed police carried out a raid in the Urewera settlements of Ruatoki and Tāneatua, as well as at other places around New Zealand, and arrested seventeen people on suspicion of terrorism activities, which turned out to be largely unfounded. Only four people were charged. One was Tame Iti. He was found to be in possession of illegal firearms and sentenced to thirty months in prison. In February 2013, after serving nine months, he was granted parole. The raids had become an embarrassment to the government.

On June 4, 2013 the New Zealand government officially apologised to Ngāi Tūhoe on behalf of the Crown for grievances spanning more than 150 years. The apology was coupled with a financial package of $170 million. As 1,400 Tūhoe gathered at parliament for the historic event, Tame Iti cruised into the grounds in a chauffeur-driven Rolls Royce. While some saw him as a showman, his grand entrance spoke volumes about his depth of feeling. His long years as an activist had finally helped bring about about a new phase for his people.

On August 13, 2014, the police apologised for actions taken during the 2007 raid, acknowledging that the way the police acted had caused a loss of mana for the iwi, and that the treatment of children and the elderly in particular had been disrespectful.

SEVEN YEARS AFTER *UREWERA MURAL* had been returned to the Āniwaniwa Visitor Centre the building was found to be leaking and had to be closed. The painting went back to Auckland Art Gallery, where it underwent further conservation. In 2011 it was exhibited at Tauranga Art Gallery, where I was director. Ngāi Tūhoe and the Department of Conservation had asked that the mural be stored close to tribal lands and in 2013 it was relocated to the Whakatāne Museum Research Centre. In March 2014 it moved again, this time to Te Whare Hou o Tūhoe, the new Tūhoe headquarters in Tāneatua, where it now hangs in the tribal chamber.

Today Tame Iti spends much of his time painting. He has had a long involvement in art, and in the 1990s had his own gallery in Auckland. In 2015 and 2016 he exhibited his paintings – unstretched and unframed like McCahon's mural – with works by a photographer, Birgit Krippner, in a thought-provoking exhibition, *Iti*, at galleries in Wellington and Auckland; the exhibition was profiled in *Art New Zealand*.

Te Kaha lives in the hills above Ōhope Beach on the fringe of Te Urewera National Park and is a respected carver of pounamu, the beautiful greenstone of Aotearoa New Zealand.

Dame Jenny Gibbs continues to enjoy an active lifestyle centred around the arts and has extensively supported the Auckland Art Gallery. She remains an avid art collector and philanthropist.

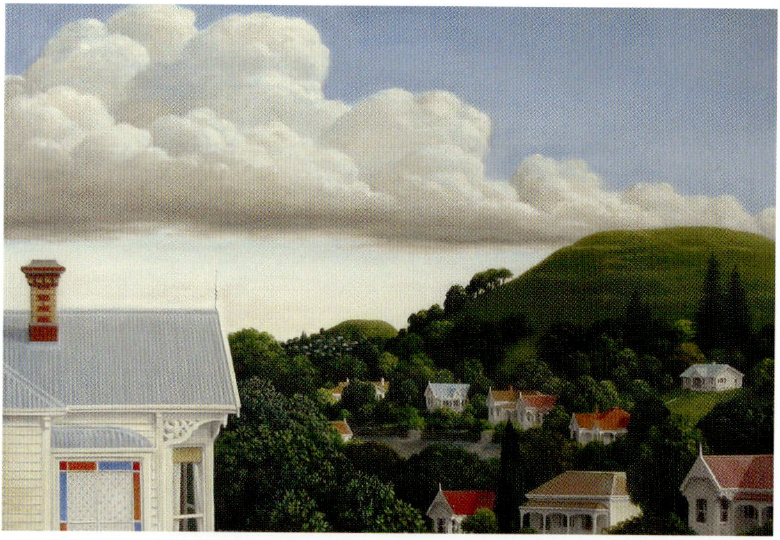

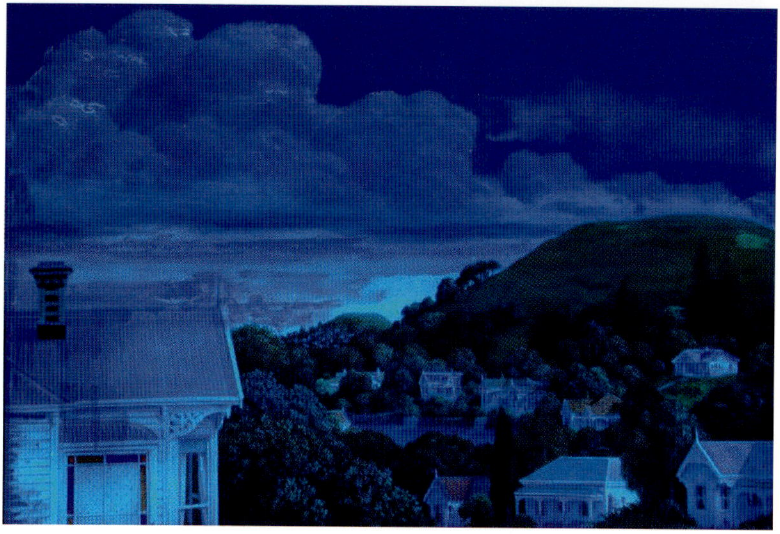

The owner of *Orange Glass*, a work by notable artist Peter Siddell for which she had paid $7,500, was dismayed to discover it was a digital print on canvas to which some brushwork had been added. TOP The 'painting' as it appeared to the naked eye. ABOVE The same work under ultraviolet light, revealing brushwork in the area of the sky and down the left-hand side. Siddell's signature had also been painted on. *Ingrid Ford photograph, Auckland Art Gallery Toi o Tamaki*

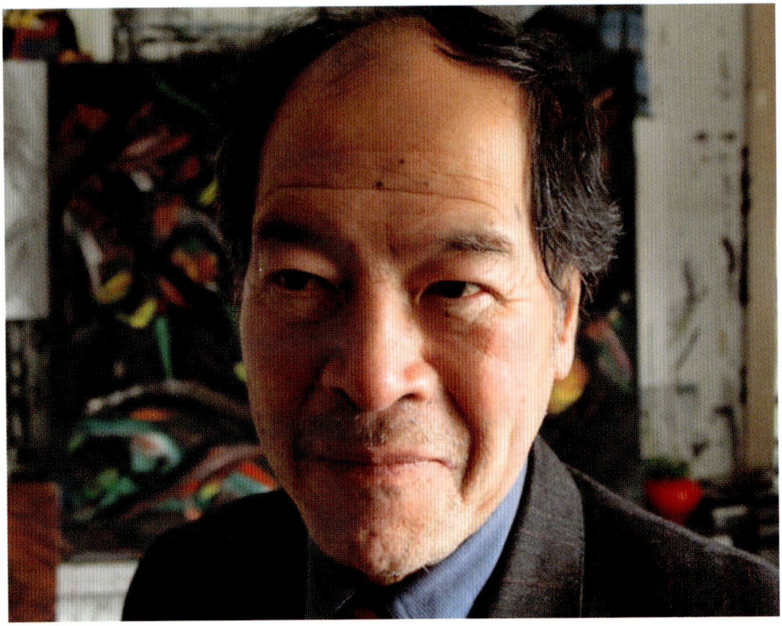

ABOVE Rossano Fan, an architect who designed a family home for artist Toss Woollaston, became enamoured of Woollaston's work and produced and marketed dozens of outright forgeries, as well as overpainting drawings by Woollaston and selling them as 'collaborations'. *Richard Riddiford Collection*

RIGHT, ABOVE *Tasman Bay*, an oil on canvas by Toss Woollaston c. 1990. Woollaston's palette of muddy ochre tones and dull greens was utterly distinctive, as was his expressive style and application of paint. *Toss Woollaston Trust/Sally Hunt Fine Art*

RIGHT A Rossano Fan painting of the same scene. The words read: 'Rossano Fan. Sketch by Woollaston 1976. Nelson in Toss & Edith's house (designed by Fan)'. Fan's forgeries were faulty – the paper was the wrong size and the palette too vivid – but many still pop up for sale. *David Hamilton Photography*

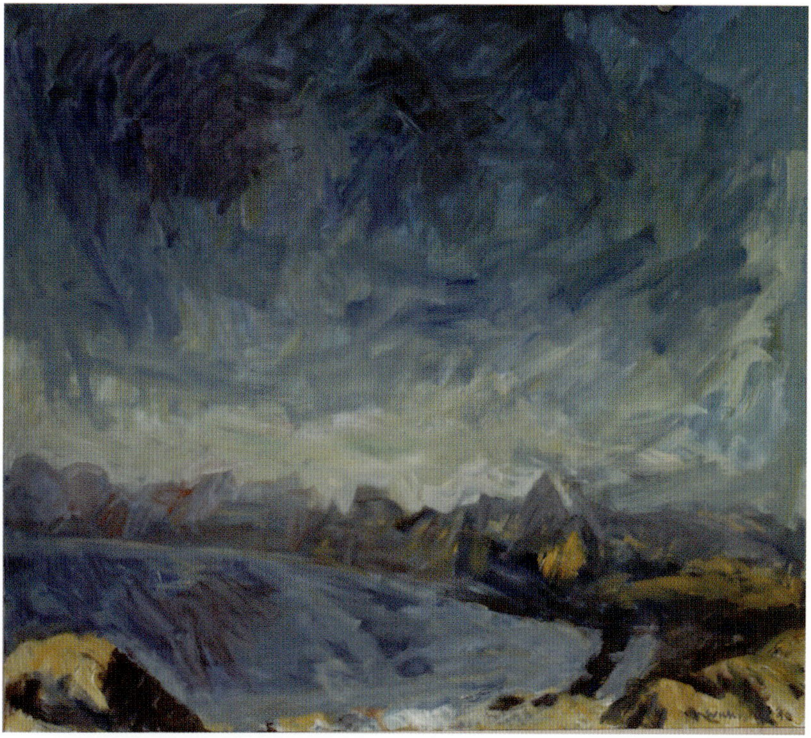

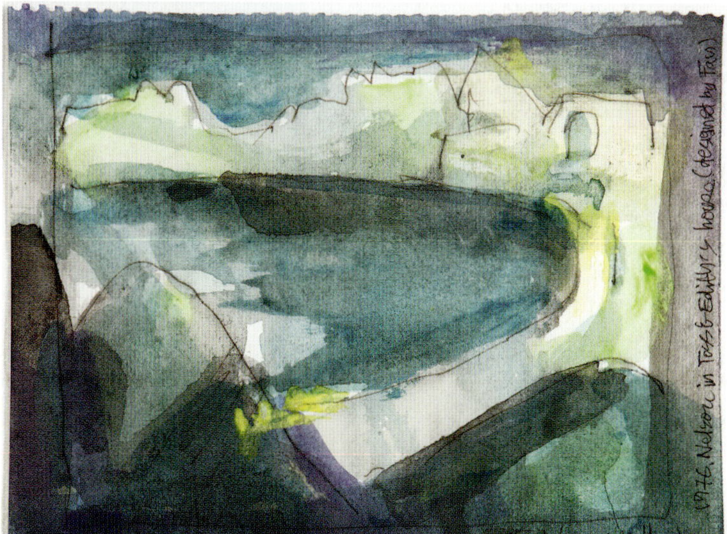
Sketch by Woollaston

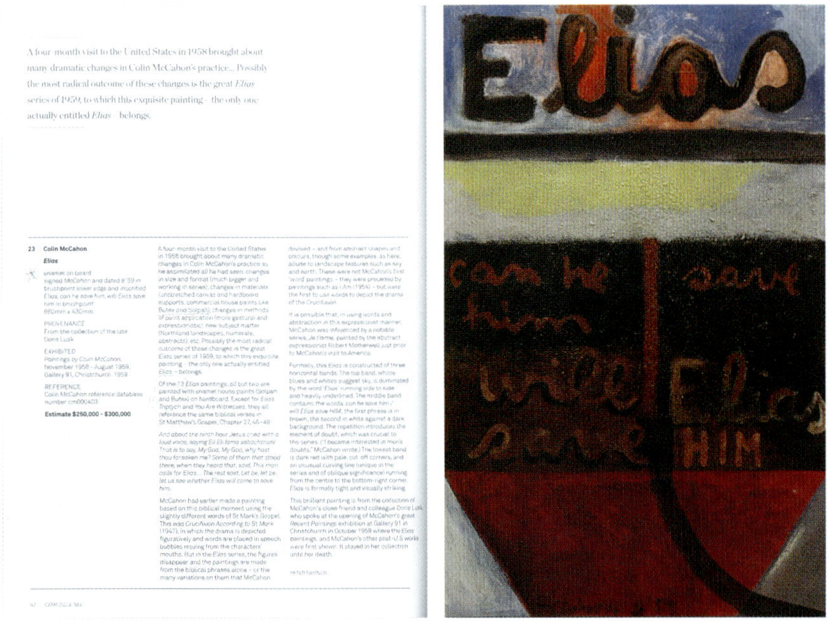

A four-month visit to the United States in 1958 brought about many dramatic changes in Colin McCahon's practice... Possibly the most radical outcome of these changes is the great *Elias* series of 1959, to which this exquisite painting – the only one actually entitled *Elias* – belongs.

23 Colin McCahon

Elias

enamel on board
signed *McCahon* and dated *8 '59* in brushpoint lower edge and inscribed *Elias, can he save him, will Elias save him* in brushpoint
660mm x 430mm

PROVENANCE
From the collection of the late Doris Lusk

EXHIBITED
Paintings by Colin McCahon, November 1958 – August 1959, Gallery 91, Christchurch, 1959

REFERENCE
Colin McCahon reference database number cm000403

Estimate $250,000 - $300,000

A four-month visit to the United States in 1958 brought about many dramatic changes in Colin McCahon's practice as he assimilated all he had seen: changes in size and format (much bigger and working in series), changes in materials (unstretched canvas and hardboard supports, commercial house paints like Butex and Solpah), changes in methods of paint application (more gestural and expressionistic), new subject matter (Northland landscapes, numerals, abstracts), etc. Possibly the most radical outcome of these changes is the great *Elias* series of 1959, to which this exquisite painting – the only one actually entitled *Elias* – belongs.

Of the 13 *Elias* paintings, all but two are painted with enamel house paints (Solpah and Butex) on hardboard. Except for *Elias Triptych* and *You Are Witnesses*, they all reference the same biblical verses in St Matthew's Gospel, Chapter 27, 46–49:

And about the ninth hour Jesus cried with a loud voice, saying Eli Eli lama sabachthani That is to say, My God, My God, why hast thou forsaken me? Some of them that stood there, when they heard that, said, This man calls for Elias... The rest said, Let be, let be, let us see whether Elias will come to save him.

McCahon had earlier made a painting based on this biblical moment using the slightly different words of St Mark's Gospel. This was *Crucifixion According to St Mark* (1947), in which the drama is depicted figuratively and words are placed in speech bubbles issuing from the characters' mouths. But in the *Elias* series, the figures disappear and the paintings are made from the biblical phrases alone – or the many variations on them that McCahon devised – and from abstract shapes and colours, though some examples, as here, allude to landscape features such as sky and earth. These were not McCahon's first 'word' paintings – they were preceded by paintings such as *I Am* (1954) – but were the first to use words to depict the drama of the Crucifixion.

It is possible that, in using words and abstraction in this expressionist manner, McCahon was influenced by a notable series, *Je t'aime*, painted by the abstract expressionist Robert Motherwell just prior to McCahon's visit to America.

Formally, this *Elias* is constructed of three horizontal bands. The top band, whose blues and whites suggest sky, is dominated by the word '*Elias*' running side to side and heavily underlined. The middle band contains the words *can he save him / will Elias save HIM*, the first phrase is in brown, the second in white against a dark background. The repetition introduces the element of doubt, which was crucial to the series. ("I became interested in men's doubts," McCahon wrote.) The lowest band is dark red with pale, cut-off corners, and an unusual curving line (unique in the series and of oblique significance) running from the centre to the bottom-right corner. *Elias* is formally tight and visually striking.

This brilliant painting is from the collection of McCahon's close friend and colleague Doris Lusk who spoke at the opening of McCahon's great *Recent Paintings* exhibition at Gallery 91 in Christchurch in October 1959 where the *Elias* paintings, and McCahon's other post-U.S works were first shown. It stayed in her collection until her death.

PETER SIMPSON

An image of *Elias*, a 1959 painting in a series by artist Colin McCahon, in the catalogue of Webb's auction house, July 2014. The painting had an estimated price of $250,000 to $300,000. People attending the auction were stunned when it was withdrawn at the last minute. No explanation has ever been given.

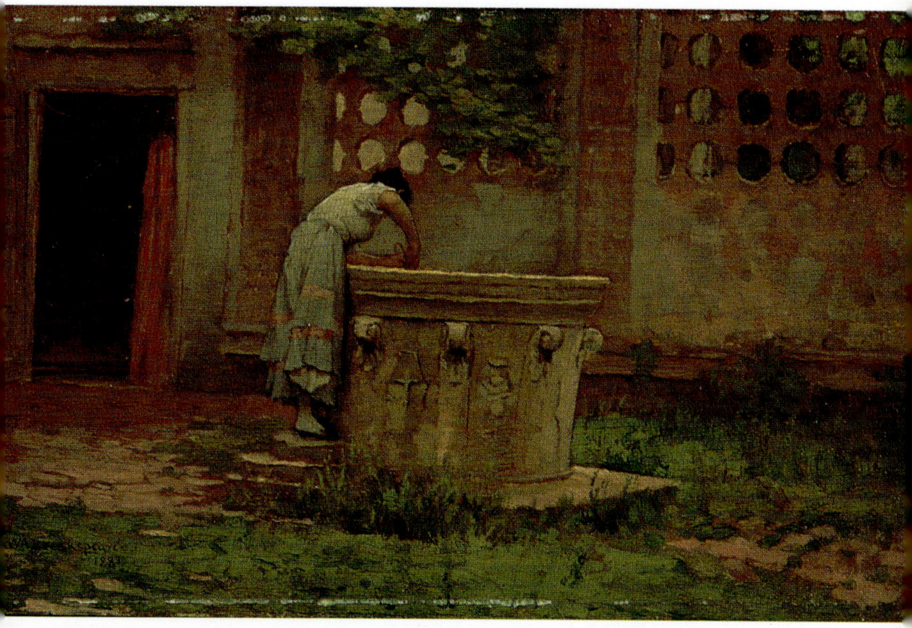

The Fountain by William Breakspeare, 1883, a small painting stolen from Christchurch's Robert McDougall Art Gallery in January 1985 and returned by police twenty-five days later. The gallery's staff were told not to ask any questions. They were intrigued to discover the painting had gained a splattering of what appeared to be tomato sauce.

Christchurch Art Gallery Te Puna o Waiwhetu

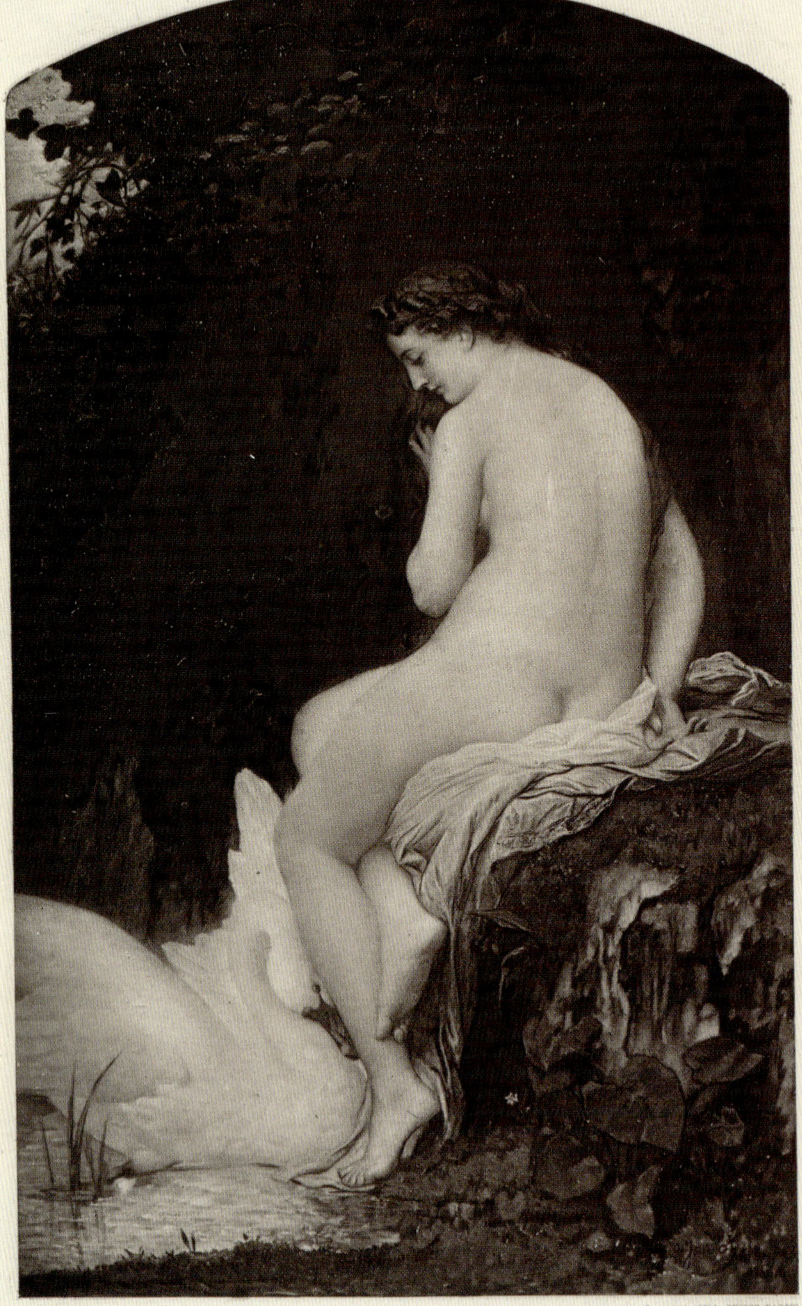

Leda and the Swan.

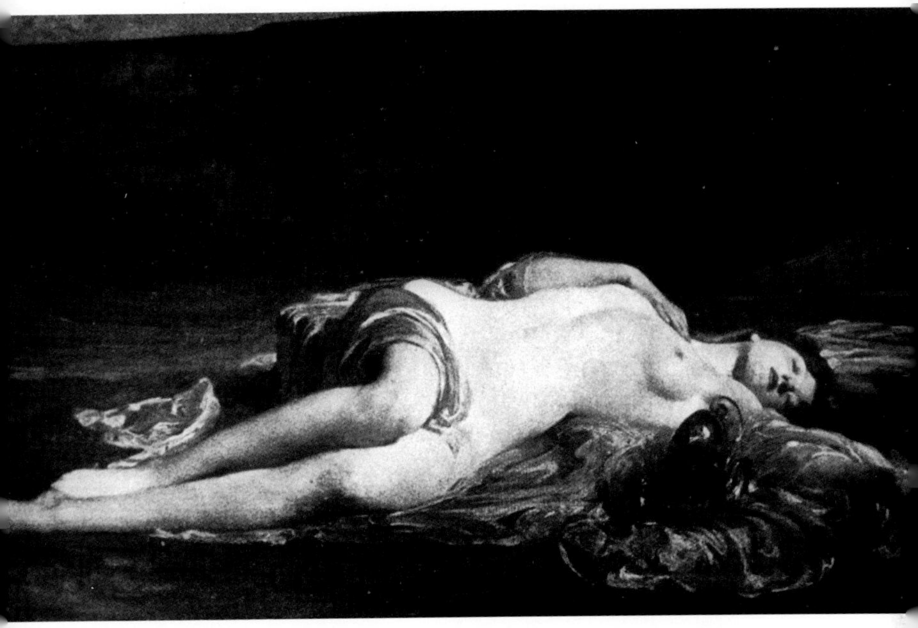

LEFT *Leda and the Swan*, a large erotic painting made around 1868 by French artist Adolphe Jourdan, presided over the South Gallery of the Robert McDougall Art Gallery after being gifted in 1932. When a curator made an inventory of the McDougall collection in 1948, the painting was not on the list. Its disappearance remains a mystery. This etching of the painting is its only record; it was found on US auction site eBay.

Tim Jones photograph, Christchurch Art Gallery Te Puna o Waiwhetu

ABOVE In classical mythology Psyche was an extraordinarily beautiful princess who was envied by the goddess Venus but ultimately married Venus's son, Cupid. This 1902 painting *Psyche* by British artist Solomon Joseph Solomon was removed from its frame and vanished from the Robert McDougall Art Gallery on the night of June 21, 1942 or in the early hours of the following day. It has never been seen again.

Christchurch Art Gallery Te Puna o Waiwhetu

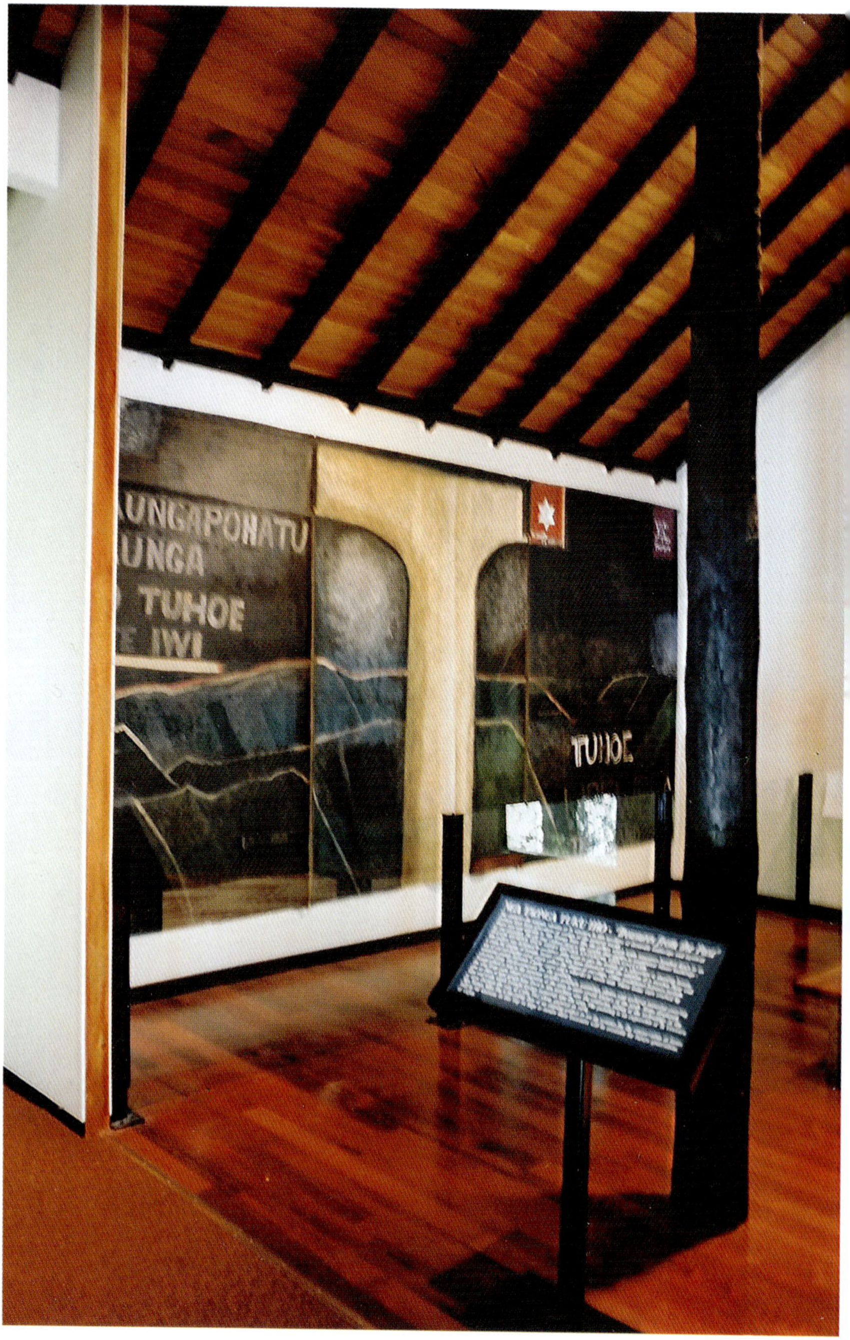
UNGAPONATU
UNGA
TUHOE
TUHOE

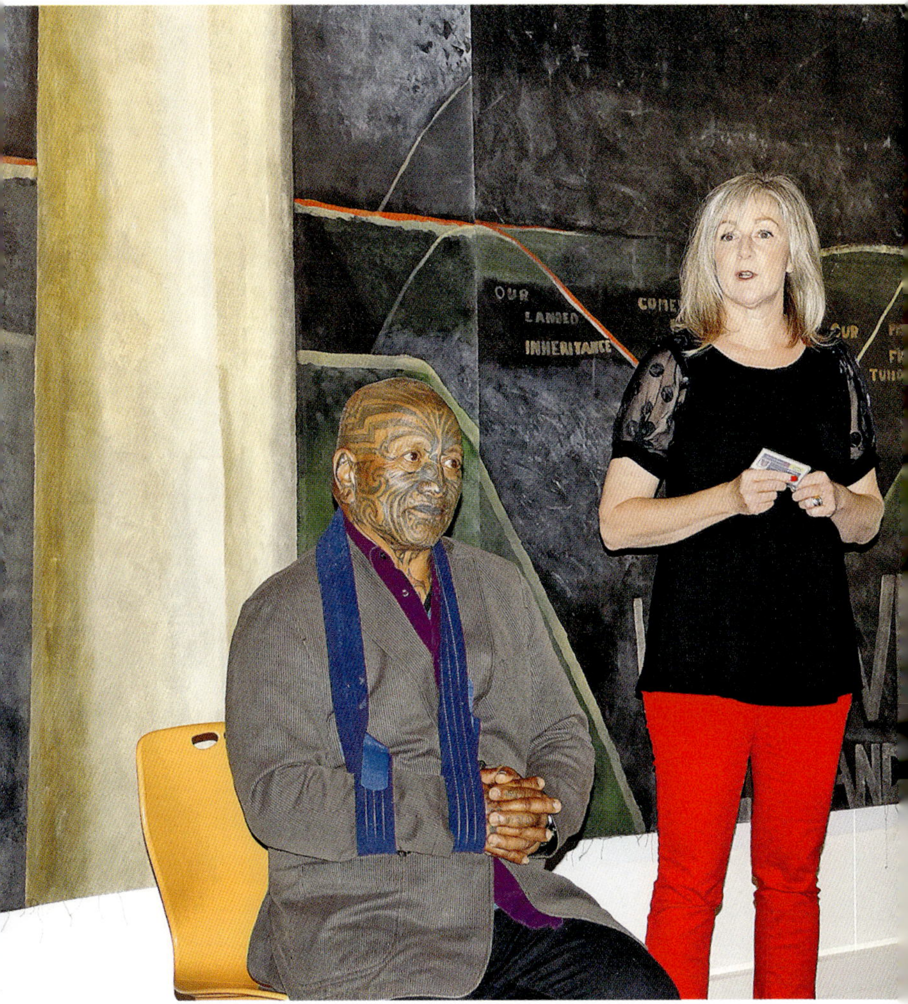

LEFT Colin McCahon's *Urewera Mural* after its return to the Āniwaniwa Visitor Centre at Waikaremoana. When it disappeared in June 1997 the police immediately suspected a political motive lay behind the theft. The painting was returned only after months of delicate negotiations involving an intermediary and had to undergo extensive conservation. *Craig Martin photograph*

ABOVE Tame Iti, a Tūhoe activist, talked about his involvement in the events leading up to the return of *Urewera Mural* to an audience at Te Kōputu a Te Whanga a Toi – the Whakatāne Library and Exhibition Centre in December 2013. *Urewera Mural* is on display behind him. On his left is Kay Boreham, museum and arts exhibition coordinator of Whakatāne District Council. *Geoff Mercer photograph, Whakatāne Beacon*

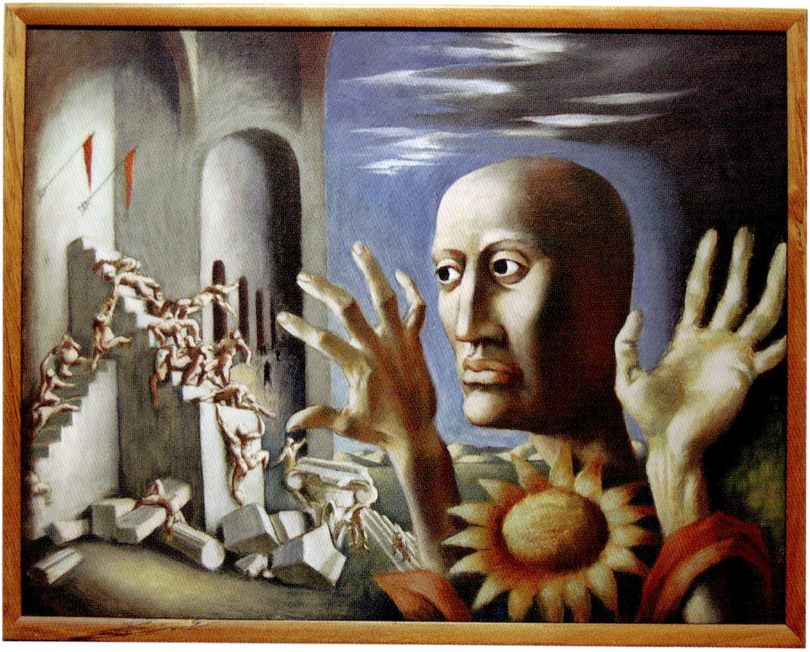

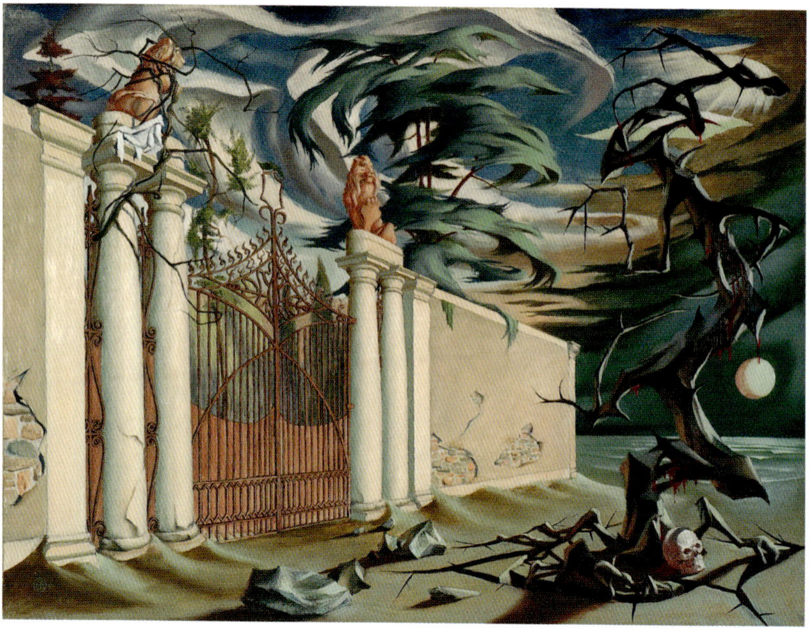

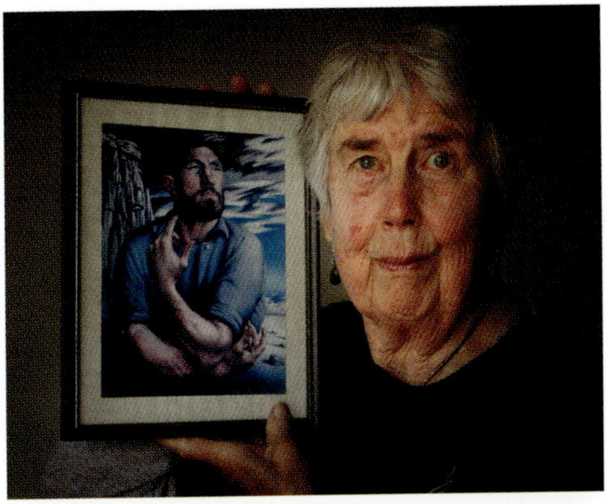

RIGHT, TOP Jacqueline Bullmore holds a print of a self-portrait by her husband Edward Bullmore. A talented and prolific artist who exhibited with surrealists such as Salvador Dalí and Joan Miró, Bullmore died young, leaving a vast collection of works, which Jacqueline entrusted to Bullmore's brother Maurice, a decision that was to have dire consequences. *Martin Hunter photograph, Fairfax New Zealand*

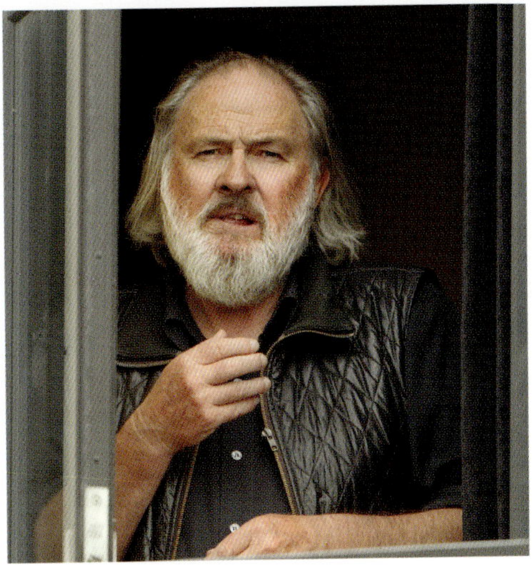

RIGHT, BELOW Pat Condon, the owner and operator of Canterbury Gallery, whom Maurice Bullmore enlisted to help him sell Edward Bullmore's artworks. Later Condon would become the sole agent. Jacqueline Bullmore received only scant payments and sales reports. Today more than 150 works are still unaccounted for. *Fairfax New Zealand*

LEFT While living in Italy in the late 1950s Edward Bullmore studied briefly under Pietro Annigoni and was influenced by his super-realist style. However, he began to move towards surrealism, painting *The Gates* (left) in Florence in 1959. *Christchurch Art Gallery/Marianna Bullmore.*

LEFT, TOP After moving to London he exhibited at dealer galleries with works such as *Transition No. 6* and he was included in the 1967 Exeter exhibition *The Enchanted Domain: Surrealist Art*. *Tauranga Art Gallery/Marianna Bullmore.*

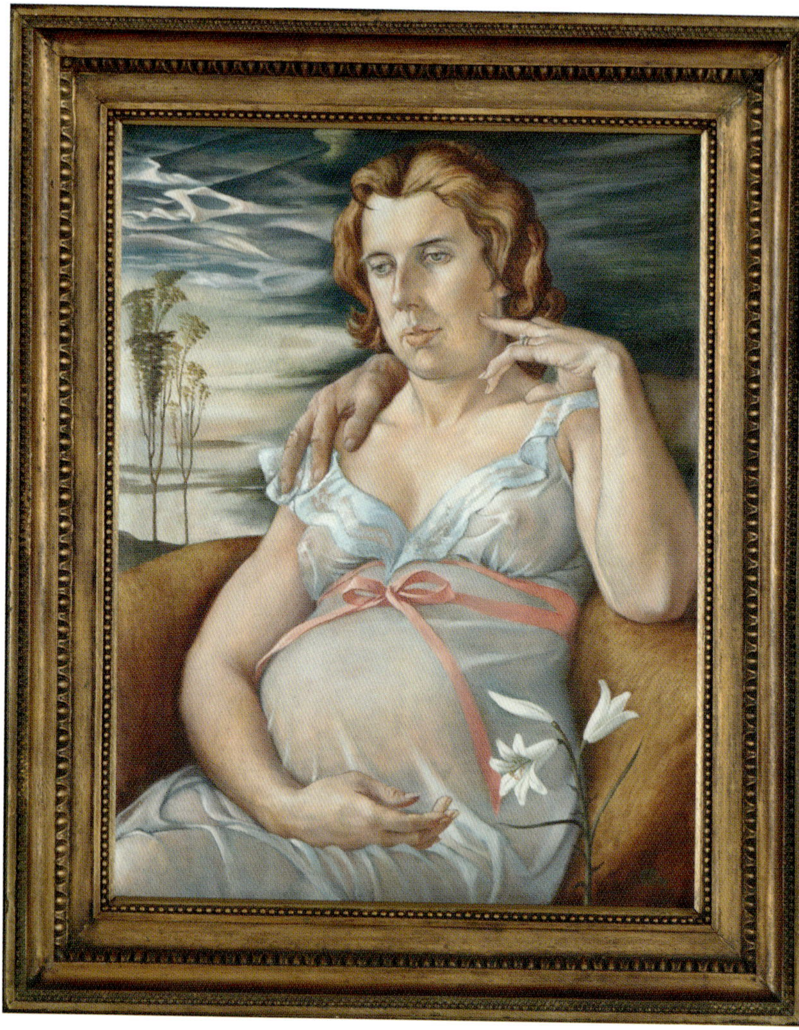

Edward Bullmore created this work, *Portrait of Jacqui* (also known as *Creation*), in 1959 while he and Jacqueline were staying in Florence and Jacqueline was pregnant with their daughter Gigliola (Lily). When Jacqueline entrusted Edward's works to Maurice Bullmore a decade after his death in 1978, there were clear instructions that this and several other private works were not for sale. In 2004 Jacqueline and her daughter Marianna were devastated to learn the painting had been sold to the Museum of New Zealand Te Papa Tongarewa.

Museum of New Zealand Te Papa Tongarewa/Marianna Bullmore

SIX

All in the family

WHEN EDWARD BULLMORE was building an art career in London during the 1960s alongside fellow New Zealand artists Pat Hanly and Ralph Hotere, he could not have imagined that fifty years later his wife and daughter would be waging a long and protracted battle against a close member of his family. Many years after her father's death, Marianna Bullmore would try without success to get the police to resolve a situation in which a great number of his artworks were missing. A letter to the Ombudsman fared no better. Her last option was to go public. After resisting this for a long time, in 2012, after considerable soul-searching, she decided to tell her story to the media.

THE ELDEST OF SEVEN CHILDREN, Edward Bullmore was born to farming parents in a remote area of Southland in 1933. Showing early artistic promise, he attended Canterbury University College School of Art before training as a teacher in Auckland.

In 1957 he took up his first position as an art teacher in Tauranga, but Italy beckoned and two years later he and his new wife Jacqueline, also an art teacher, headed to Florence.

Numerous sketches and paintings depict the couple's idyllic six months in Italy. Bullmore studied briefly under Pietro Annigoni, an artist known for his portraits of royalty, movie stars and public figures. While his principal objective was to acquire Annigoni's tempera grassa technique, which used a hybrid glaze of egg tempera and oil paint, he was also influenced by Annigoni's super-realist style. Increasingly interested in surrealism, he produced a small group of extraordinary 'transitional' paintings such as *The Thorn Tree*, in which he used his own image in a crucifixion scene.

In January 1960 the couple's Italian visas expired and they moved to London, where they would live for a decade, enjoying what would be, in retrospect, the heyday of Edward Bullmore's artistic career, with exhibitions at London dealer galleries and in several Commonwealth group exhibitions. The highlight was his inclusion in a 1967 Exeter exhibition, *The Enchanted Domain: Surrealist Art*, which consolidated his position as a surrealist exhibiting alongside artists such as Dalí, Miro and de Chirico.

In 1969, wanting to give their three school-aged children a New Zealand upbringing, the couple returned and set up home in Rotorua. Bullmore's art proved too edgy for local tastes.[16] It was often raw, both in subjects and materials, and he regularly painted nudes. To provide an income for the family he taught at Rotorua Boys' High School, where his students nicknamed him 'Gentle Ben'.

In 1978, at only forty-five, Bullmore died suddenly of a heart attack, leaving not only a widow and three teenage children but a large body of work – around five hundred paintings, sculptures, prints, drawings and ceramics. This vast collection presented a problem for Jacqueline Bullmore. With only a small widow's pension she could not pay to have the works housed long-term, let alone insure and maintain them in good condition. Nor could she readily dispose of the collection or any part of it in Rotorua, which had no specialist dealer galleries.

In 1991 she appointed Edward's youngest brother Maurice Bullmore as guardian of and sales agent for the collection. A legal contract was drawn up, outlining Maurice's responsibilities. He was to care for and provide 'safe custody' of the works, have the collection valued, and exhibit and sell works. As agent he would take forty percent commission on any works sold, a generous figure given that he had no gallery overheads to cover, and was a builder with no background in the visual arts. The contract identified a number of works that had particular significance to Jacqueline and her children and were not to be sold.

The entire collection was picked up from Rotorua by Maurice Bullmore on March 15 and transported to Christchurch, where it was stored in a warehouse at 84 Lichfield Street. To help him sell the works, Maurice soon involved another party. Pat Condon was a well-known dealer and the owner and operator of Canterbury Gallery, housed in a converted villa at 48 Papanui Road. Over the next few years Bullmore's works would be exhibited on several occasions at Condon's gallery.

Almost from the outset, the family struggled to get answers out of Maurice Bullmore as to where the works were being stored, and how many had been sold, to whom and at what price. Whenever Jacqueline inquired she was fobbed off with excuses. Usually Maurice claimed to be a little short of cash but said he would pay her in time. The money rarely arrived.

It would later become clear that Bullmore and Condon were selling Edward Bullmore's paintings and sculptures for well below their market value. Maurice Bullmore appeared to have little or no regard to their value and merely wanted to make quick sales. In 1996, for example, he sold a 1961 painting, *Market Faces No. 1*, for $4,000. Eight years later it was resold for $45,000. A 1996 Canterbury Gallery sales record showed Maurice Bullmore and Pat Condon taking fifty percent of sales proceeds – ten percent more than they were contractually entitled to – and remitting the other fifty percent to Jacqueline. Sometimes they kept even more. When *Market Faces No. 1* was sold, Jacqueline received only $2,000, not the $2,400 to which she was entitled.

Jacqueline increasingly suspected Maurice Bullmore of not presenting accurate sales invoices, not passing on her full share of the proceeds, and sometimes not reporting sales at all. Feeling she could no longer trust him, in 1997 she cancelled their agreement. She decided to entrust Pat Condon with the collection, and signed a legal agreement with him and his lawyer, Paul Kellar. Condon would sell the works through his Canterbury Gallery, where he represented a number of artists. The contract turned out to be strongly biased in Condon's favour. Jacqueline's lawyer, Malcolm Haycock, drafted a new one but Condon avoided signing it. Unbeknownst to Jacqueline, he also continued working with Maurice Bullmore.

JACQUELINE VISITED CHRISTCHURCH regularly but Condon steadfastly refused to show her any of the works, or engage in conversations about sales. In May 1999 her luck seemed to be about to change. Condon informed her he was negotiating a major sale of twenty works to a collective known as the Canterbury Collection

Trust. The newly established trust was purportedly a group of collectors who wanted to invest in art.

For two years Condon strung Jacqueline along, providing sales receipts as evidence of purchases by the trust, and mentioning meetings with its members. Later, as further proof of his bona fides, he told her he had employed a full-time researcher to work on a book about Bullmore.

In 2001 there was more news. The Canterbury Collection Trust now wanted to purchase the entire collection of Edward's works for $250,000. Condon's commission would be fifty percent. Like many of Condon's schemes, the sale never materialised. It could not do so: the Canterbury Collection Trust did not exist.

IN 2002 MARIANNA BULLMORE, the youngest of Edward and Jacqueline Bullmore's children and herself an artist, returned from overseas. Two years later she began to help Jacqueline take legal action to retrieve her husband's works. They engaged a Christchurch lawyer, Garth Gallaway, a passionate art-lover who worked tirelessly on the case with little remuneration.

The collection turned out to be scattered around Christchurch. Most works were repossessed from Yvonne Fine Arts, a new gallery run by Condon's wife. All works collected were placed in storage at City Art Depot, a private, professionally run facility. For Jacqueline and Marianna, who had not seen the collection for over a decade, the process was highly emotional. By then I had come to know the two women and on one occasion I accompanied Marianna to Maurice Bullmore's home in Linwood to pick up some of Edward's works. The house was extremely damp, and it was immediately obvious the paintings had not been cared for and had suffered damage.

To make matters worse, it soon became apparent that a lot of works were missing. There was no record of where they might be. The story of the last few years slowly began to emerge. Maurice Bullmore and Pat Condon had not only sold works without declaring the sales to Jacqueline, they had used works to pay off debts, and had exchanged works for those of other artists and other collectors. On other occasions Maurice had simply given them away; for instance, he had given his daughter one of Edward's works as a graduation present.

IN THE EARLY YEARS OF HIS MARRIAGE Edward had painted Jacqueline on numerous occasions, creating works that ranged from large-scale surrealist nudes to representational drawings of her working at the kitchen bench. Three portraits stood out as milestones in his artistic development, each distinctly different in style.

The most impressive was *Portrait of Jacqui*, a work in egg tempera and dry pigment on canvas board, 948 x 780 mm, which he had painted in 1959 during the couple's stay in Florence.[17] Jacqueline is in the last stages of pregnancy. She caresses her stomach, her naked body clearly visible through her gossamer nightgown. The painting is rich in symbolism, particularly the inclusion of a lily, a common symbol in Renaissance Annunciation scenes. Here it references the Christmas lily that flowers in the New Zealand summer. The baby was due in December, and the unopened bud denoted the impending birth. When the baby was born she was named Gigliola, the Italian word for lily. The work, therefore, had huge sentimental value for the family.

During the early 1990s this painting, along with six others, was cared for by Gigliola, who is now known as Lily England. In 1996

Lily was living in shared accommodation and the paintings were stored in a cupboard. Unable to afford insurance and feeling the responsibility of looking after the valuable works was too great, she decided to hand over all seven to her uncle, Maurice Bullmore, for safekeeping. She prepared a document itemising each work and stating that on November 24, 1996 she had delivered them to Bullmore's store at Lichfield Street. The document, dated December 1, included the statement: 'I have directed Uncle Maurice Bullmore that these works are not for sale unless authorisation is given at a later date.' To ensure her directions were followed she sent copies of the document not only to Maurice but also to Jacqueline, Marianna, and her brother Oliver Bullmore.

In 2001, unsure whether Maurice Bullmore had told Pat Condon of all the family works that were not to be sold, Jacqueline gave him a copy of the list. As Bullmore had produced three major portraits of Jacqueline – *Portrait of Jacquie*, *Jacqueline* and *Portrait of Jacqui* – to avoid any confusion she had written 'pregnant' in brackets next to *Portrait of Jacqui*.

In 2004, when Jacqueline and Marianna retrieved works from Condon, they were shocked to find *Portrait of Jacqui* was missing. After numerous telephone calls and letters they discovered the two men had sold it to Te Papa through a private dealer the previous year. They were devastated to learn that the intensely private work was now in a public gallery, and had no idea what had happened to the money Te Papa had paid. It would emerge that the men had pocketed the whole $150,000, minus a small commission to the dealer. Perhaps by using another dealer to sell the painting, Condon had been trying to distance himself from the transaction. When Jacqueline's lawyer questioned him he initially denied any knowledge of the sale. Later, in fear of being exposed, he would pay Jacqueline the entire $150,000 in two instalments.

JACQUELINE AND MARIANNA BULLMORE made two other disturbing discoveries in 2004. When Edward Bullmore died in November 1978 he had left behind unfinished works. These included *Mamaku Earth and Sky No. 6*, the last in a series of sculptures he had been working on all that year. In his final months he had cut back his teaching to four days a week and each Friday had travelled to the Mamaku district, about 25 kilometres west of Lake Rotorua, to draw the rugged landscape, which fascinated him with its large rocky outcrops.

The *Mamaku* works were brutal, framed with rough-sawn timbers. The palette was earthy and the works had a rawness far removed from the large colourful forms of Bullmore's previous series, *Icons*. The canvases had ceramic inserts. The last two pieces abandoned the traditional rectangular picture frame altogether and relied on parts of Bentwood chairs to frame and structure unusual shapes.

In *No. 6* the Bentwood chair frames were arranged in almost a figure eight configuration. An experimental work, the sculpture combined the New Zealand landscape tradition with the found objects intrinsic to Bullmore's London works. It and the fifth Mamaku work represented a significant new direction.

When they received *Mamaku Earth and Sky No. 6*, Marianna and Jacqueline were dismayed to see it had been vandalised. The unpainted area of canvas now contained a meaningless jumble of words in blue biro, including 'War? What is it good for?' surrounded by swastikas. After matching handwriting samples, the women discovered this was the work of Maurice Bullmore. A report from a conservator indicated that the quantity of biro ink on the canvas precluded the work from being restored. It was another bitter blow for the family.

Also unfinished at the time of Edward Bullmore's death was *Astroform No. 14*. The *Astroform* series had been particularly successful for the artist, who had developed these 'shaped paintings' – canvases stretched over wooden armatures – while living in London. Large exuberant works, each with a unique form and a sexually suggestive quality, they had attracted much attention and critical acclaim.

Astroform No. 14 had been among the works entrusted to Maurice Bullmore and Pat Condon. When Jacqueline and Marianna retrieved it, they immediately saw it had been 'completed'. There is only a small market for unfinished works and Condon must have hoped that having *Astroform No. 14* finished would make it more saleable. He had commissioned well-known artist Michael Smither to finish the work. Smither had completed the painting in quintessential Canterbury colours of red and black. An investigation proved the paint could not be removed.

I spoke with Michael Smither about his part in the affair. He told me the painting was in poor condition when he accepted the invitation to finish it. Part of his work was to be remedial. Pat Condon had sent him drawings that had nothing to do with the particular work and were of little use. In the 1960s, when Bullmore was living in London, his work had been collected by the film director Stanley Kubrick, and two of his shaped canvases had featured in Kubrick's 1971 movie *A Clockwork Orange*. Familiar with these works, Smither had set about finishing *Astroform No. 14* in a manner he believed to be in keeping with Bullmore's palette. It had taken him nearly six months and he had never been paid.

Subsequently Smither would himself become a victim of Condon's questionable business practices: three of his paintings 'disappeared' while in the custody of the dealer.

EARLY IN 2006 JACQUELINE BULLMORE was driving through the hillside suburb of Cashmere in Christchurch to visit friends when curiosity took her down Kidson Terrace, where Maurice Bullmore had built a house in the 1980s. She had once known the owners of the house, and decided to knock on the door to see if they were still living there. When the door opened she was struck dumb: one of her husband's works, *Icon No. 3*, was hanging inside.

A large sculptural piece made of stretched canvas and containing a blue ceramic insert in the shape of a cross, *Icon No. 3* had been made by Edward Bullmore in Rotorua in 1974. One of his most impressive and ambitious works of the time, it had been the sole one chosen to hang at his funeral at St Luke's Anglican Church in Rotorua in November 1978 and so had strong sentimental value for the family. Jacqueline referred to it as 'The Blue Cross of Sorrow' and had several times asked Maurice Bullmore to return it to her, without success. In 2004 her lawyer, Garth Gallaway, had also contacted Bullmore and insisted the work be returned, with a similar lack of success.

The people in the house appeared taken aback by Jacqueline's visit. They were, they eventually admitted, storing the work for Maurice Bullmore and would be happy to hand it over. Garth Gallaway quickly arranged to have *Icon No. 3* uplifted, but the saga was not over. Jacqueline, who was living in a small flat, had neither the space nor the funds to care for and insure *Icon No. 3*, which was over a metre square and 300 mm deep. She gifted the work to the

Tauranga Art Gallery Trust, which had been founded eight years earlier with the goal of setting up a gallery in the growing city. The trust paid eight hundred dollars to have a crate built to transport the work safely north from Christchurch, and while this was taking place the work was stored at the City Art Depot.

Around ten o'clock on the night of June 6, 2006 Maurice Bullmore scaled the depot's perimeter fence, crossed the yard and attempted to break a window. When alarms went off he clambered up the exterior staircase in an attempt to enter the building another way. The police arrived soon afterwards and caught him on the roof with his gloves still on.

Charged with burglary, Bullmore entered a guilty plea. His lawyer, Tim Mackenzie, stated in mitigation that Bullmore had once owned the painting and felt he was still the rightful owner. 'He has gone about it the wrong way,' Mackenzie said, 'but it was more of a message he wanted to send than a criminal act.' In fact Maurice Bullmore had never owned *Icon No. 3*. He was sentenced to one hundred hours of community service for his 'message'. The work duly arrived in Tauranga and went into storage pending the opening of the gallery in 2007.

Meanwhile there had been another twist in the story. In April 2006 Tauranga Art Gallery had received a letter from a Mr V stating he was the lawful owner of *Icon No. 3* and wanted it returned as soon as possible.[18] This came as a complete surprise since the work, then still in the depot, had been formally gifted to the gallery. We immediately sought legal advice: as a charitable trust and public gallery we needed to be sure the work's provenance was watertight.

Meanwhile Mr V became increasingly impatient and agitated. 'If you decide to retain the painting knowing I am the owner,' he wrote, 'matters will arise where you have continued to keep property which now you [know] is owned by me.' He also made several phone calls. Somehow he managed to get my personal mobile phone number and his calls made me very nervous.

It turned out that Mr V was a well-known criminal.[19] Maurice Bullmore had sold *Icon No. 3* to him in 1993 for $15,000, considerably less than its value on the open market. Mr V was interested in the artwork only as an investment he could quickly turn into cash when needed, and had been happy to have it sequestered at the Christchurch house. This explained why Maurice Bullmore had been so desperate to retrieve the work from the City Art Depot.

After viewing the documentation, Garth Gallaway confirmed that Mr V was the rightful owner. Jacqueline had no choice but to send a letter to Tauranga Art Gallery stating she could not legally gift the work after all. On May 22, 2007, Mr V, accompanied by his wife and two school-aged children, arrived in Tauranga after driving up from Christchurch. There appeared to be a sense of urgency. I suggested he might like to purchase the crate to transport the work safely but he quickly signed the documents and slung the large painting into the back of his station wagon. I asked if he would consider lending the work to the gallery for a forthcoming Edward Bullmore retrospective exhibition. He was not remotely interested and made it clear he was selling the work. His parting shot was that he already had a buyer lined up in Australia.

Like many in the world of visual arts I regularly check to see what is for sale on the New Zealand online auction site Trade Me. Among an abundance of amateur art, every now and then something attracts my attention. In August 2007 *Icon No. 3* popped up.

The asked-for starting bid was $95,000. Works of this calibre are usually put up for sale by professionally run auction houses and featured in their glossy catalogues. It wasn't long before people began to ask the seller questions, including about the work's provenance and the controversy surrounding it. When no bids were received, *Icon No. 3* was offered at a 'buy now' price of $170,000 but before the auction had run its course the painting was withdrawn.

Three years later Tauranga Art Gallery managed to buy *Icon No. 3* from Mr V for $20,000. The work had come full circle: it would now join the major public collection of Edward Bullmore's work and give some closure to his family.

IN SEPTEMBER 2007 MARIANNA BULLMORE approached the police in Tauranga and reported that more than 150 of her father's artworks entrusted to Pat Condon were still missing or unaccounted for. She was advised to gather all the information she could. To build a case the police would need evidence.

Marianna spent a year compiling detailed records of her father's works. Fortunately, Jacqueline had kept every piece of paperwork from the start of her dealings with Maurice Bullmore in 1990. This included correspondence, exhibition catalogues, and the few sales receipts she had received. In February 2008, to give the police an idea of the magnitude of the case and the market value of the collection, she also paid to have every work valued.[20]

In December that year Marianna forwarded the material in three large ring binders to the Christchurch police fraud squad. It included a letter from Pat Condon dated July 30, 2004, after it had been found that numerous works placed in his care were missing:

Dear Jacqueline and Marianna,
I am VERY VERY SORRY.
Kind regards
Pat Condon.

In May 2010, having heard nothing and becoming increasingly concerned that Maurice Bullmore and Pat Condon were not being investigated, Marianna contacted the Christchurch police. She was surprised and annoyed to discover that the detective in charge of the case was now working only part-time in order to pursue a career change as a beauty therapist. She felt the police had strung her along into believing they were working steadily on the case, when in fact there had been little progress. It now appeared Maurice Bullmore might escape culpability on medical grounds. The detective explained by email that she had spoken with Bullmore's doctor at Sydenham Medical Centre and been told that Bullmore had advanced dementia and was spending a lot of time at Hillmorton, a hospital providing specialist mental health services. She was, she said, unsure whether he understood what a caution was.

Meanwhile, the 'other chap' (Pat Condon) had been avoiding her, missing appointments on the grounds he was too busy. Although the detective admitted having interviewed Condon once, there was no record of this. He had, she said, been given two weeks to front up to the police station or be charged. In the event, he didn't show up and wasn't charged.

On August 10, 2011 Detective Mike Bridgman notified Marianna that the police would not be pressing charges. The case, he said, was heavily reliant on further interviews with Pat Condon and Maurice Bullmore. Bullmore was in no state of mind to be interviewed and

Condon had declined on the basis that he had already cooperated by being interviewed once. 'The inability to interview those two individuals,' Bridgman wrote, 'leaves us in a position where the evidence we have is insufficient to establish a prima facie case in terms of any offences that may have been committed by these two individuals.'

It had been four years since Marianna had first approached the police and by now the force had more pressing priorities, including the aftermath of the devastating Christchurch earthquakes of September 2010 and February 2011. With 150-plus works still missing, money still owed, and the police uninterested in pursuing the case, she approached *The Sunday Star-Times.*

A media storm erupted, and not all of it focused on the works that were still missing. There was also considerable interest in the purchase by the national museum of *Portrait of Jacqui*. The newspaper's headline read: 'EXCLUSIVE – Te Papa caught up in major art scandal'. Although Te Papa had bought the painting in good faith from a reputable dealer, questions remained. Why had the museum not fully investigated the painting's provenance – by, for example, contacting the family, a reasonably common way of finding out more about the content and provenance of an artwork? And why had it simply accepted the asking price of $150,000 when a larger work by Edward Bullmore, *The Family*, had sold in 2002 at Webb's auction house in Auckland for only $100,000? It emerged that, as a sweetener, the dealer had suggested that a 1959 companion piece, *Self Portrait*, would be made available within a year and the two portraits would sit brilliantly together. This never eventuated.[21]

After the *Sunday Star-Times* article, another instance of non-payment came to the fore. John Gow, owner of Gow Langsford

Gallery in Auckland, admitted he had not paid Jacqueline when he had sold one of Edward Bullmore's works, *Log Pile* (1978) during a clearout in 2007 after he bought the business from his parents. The painting, with its Rotorua connection, had sold at auction to the Rotorua Energy Charitable Trust for $5,392. Even though Marianna Bullmore had been in contact with the gallery over ownership of the work, the words 'vendor unknown' were recorded against it in the gallery's records. Perhaps not wanting to tarnish his good reputation as a dealer, John Gow paid the family immediately.

Another case soon hit the headlines. In early 2009 Jacqueline had been about to travel overseas and actually waiting at the airport when she had been approached by two Christchurch art auctioneers, John McCormack and Rob McKellar, with an offer to pay her for her husband's painting *Perseus*. Created in 1959 when Bullmore was in Florence, the painting depicted *Perseus with the Head of Medusa*, a bronze sculpture made by Benvenuto Cellini in 1545 that stands in Loggia dei Lanzi in Florence's Piazza della Signoria.

The painting had a chequered history. At some stage Maurice Bullmore had sold it and ten other Bullmore works to a Christchurch publican for $45,000, much less than their market value, and given none of the proceeds to Jacqueline. McCormack and McKellar had subsequently bought the painting and several others from the publican. Now aware that ownership of many of Bullmore's works was being disputed, they wanted Jacqueline to sign a document giving them full ownership of it 'and associated artworks' in exchange for $5,000. Short of funds, Jacqueline accepted.

McCormack and McKellar sent the painting almost immediately to Auckland's International Art Centre, where it sold at auction for $42,560. The successful bidder was reported to be David Kirk, a former All Black, who had until recently been chief executive of Fairfax Media in Australia.

TODAY, OWNERS OF BULLMORE WORKS are often nervous about trying to sell them. Many who purchased works during the Maurice Bullmore/Pat Condon years had assumed that because of Maurice Bullmore's family connections the works were above board but the news stories have created doubt. While I was writing this book I was, for example, contacted by a man in Christchurch who has four works he purchased in the 1990s from Maurice Bullmore. He has a receipt for them from M Bullmore, but does he really own them?

In 2006 Jacqueline and Marianna Bullmore gifted 287 of the Edward Bullmore works that they had retrieved in 2004 with the help of Garth Gallaway to the permanent collection of Tauranga Art Gallery. Today the artist's legacy lives on in the city he enjoyed as a young artist and teacher. The 150 or more lost works remain lost; Jacqueline and Marianna believe Maurice Bullmore and Pat Condon sold them and pocketed the money, or in some cases bartered works for other goods. Today in her eighties, Jacqueline, who should be comfortably off from sales of her husband's works, lives in a council bedsit. The men who defrauded her have never been punished, other than by public exposure in a newspaper article.

EIGHT

Lot No. 60

A CENTURY AGO NEW ZEALAND prided itself on having two major painters of Māori portraits: as well as Charles Goldie there was Gottfried Lindauer. Whereas Goldie had been born in Auckland in 1870 and as a young man had studied art at Académie Julian in Paris and anatomy at the École des Beaux-Arts, Lindauer had been born in Bohemia, a region in today's Czechia, trained in art at a Viennese academy, and arrived in New Zealand, dodging service in the Austro-Hungarian army, in 1874.

The portraits produced by both men, revered at the time and still today, are significant not only artistically but also for what they record about Māori history. For iwi they are direct links to whakapapa, and provide information about aspects of culture such as tā moko, traditional tattooing. Ngahiraka Mason, the former curator of Māori art at Auckland Art Gallery, noted of Lindauer that his portraits had advanced the value placed on Māori portraiture. 'Initially produced for the use and scrutiny of Pākehā and, on occasion, for the enjoyment of Māori who commissioned portraits,'

Mason wrote in a 2011 survey of New Zealand art in the gallery, 'they have become a valued record of the colony's history as well as being cherished by descendants.'

Sometime in the 1890s Lindauer painted the Tainui chief Kewene Te Haho, who was then in his eighties. The portrait, oil on canvas, was 745 x 600 mm. The title, painted in red on the back of the canvas, read: 'Portrait of Kewene Te Haho, Dominant Chief of the Ngatinaho Tribe at Makaka-Aotea Harbour, West Coast of New Zealand.' In 1902 the portrait was formally acknowledged by the chief's son, Ratapu Kewene, to be of his father, and in 1915 it was gifted to the Auckland Art Gallery by a private collector.

In 2001 a second Lindauer portrait of Kewene Te Haho was purchased for the collection of Trust Waikato, to be exhibited at the Waikato Museum Te Whare Taonga o Waikato in Hamilton. This was an important acquisition: Waikato is the home of Tainui. Many of the chief's descendants began regularly visiting the museum to pay homage to their ancestor and great-great-grandfather.

In January 2012, during a visit to the museum, a Whanganui artist called Peter Ireland was drawn to the Lindauer portrait. He later explained to a reporter from *The New Zealand Herald*: 'Everything … was wrong. The lighting in it, the anatomical treatment of the ear and head … [and] there was no ageing on the painting.' Ireland not only had extensive knowledge of paint application through his work as an artist, he was also familiar with Lindauer's work as the Whanganui Regional Museum had an extensive collection of Lindauer portraits.[22]

Ireland felt extremely suspicious about the work's authenticity. He alerted the museum staff and asked for an investigation to be carried out. The accusation that the portrait was not by Lindauer's own hand was taken very seriously and a process was put in place to gather all the relevant information. Given that a decade had elapsed since the painting had been purchased, investigating its provenance was going to take some time. In the intervening years the membership of the Waikato Trust's board and staff had changed completely and Stuart Stubbs, the art adviser at the time the painting was acquired, was no longer in the role.

As a first step the museum consulted Roger Blackley, an art historian at Victoria University who specialises in New Zealand colonial art. When he inspected the work, Blackley noted that the surface had an unusual granular quality, almost as though sand had been added to the paint. Also dubious was what Blackley described as the painting's 'factual quality'. The handling of the brushwork was too rough. The detail on the cloak, for example, was not sufficiently fine for a Lindauer work.

Blackley also scrutinised every detail of the back of the paintings; there were inconsistencies, such as newish tacks that had been used to attach the canvas to the stretcher. He concluded that the painting, for which the trust had paid $121,000 at auction, was 'a calculated forgery of a highly sophisticated nature, which for over a decade has successfully duped a range of experts'.

In October 2012 a complaint was laid with the police. Stuart Stubbs was in disbelief, telling a reporter in January 2013 that neither he nor the International Art Centre, which had sold the painting, had any doubt it was by Lindauer, although they were not able to provide any evidence of its authenticity.

'The auctioneer does have provenance,' he stated, adding, 'Of course, although major art houses go to great lengths to authenticate major works offered, they can only go so far. To them [there were] no problems with the look of the work, nor with the structure of the frame, stretcher or labelling.'

After carrying out some initial questioning, the police realised they had little to go on. The eleven years that had passed since the work was purchased made it difficult, even impossible, to hold anyone accountable, and as the person who had produced the fake was unknown there was no one to charge.

Portrait of Kewene Te Haho was dispatched to the conservation department of Auckland Art Gallery for testing. Sarah Hillary, the principal conservator, told me that in many ways the portrait was 'frighteningly well done'. The artist, whoever he or she was, had gone to some trouble to make it look like the real thing. But overall there were just too many inconsistencies for it to be a Lindauer.

'The painting is very skilfully painted and closely resembles the Auckland Art Gallery painting of the same sitter,' Hillary reported. 'However, there are some important inconsistencies with Lindauer's known technique and what one would expect of a painting of that age.' These included opaque paint with sand-like material added; a random fluorescent blue dot pattern over the surface, visible under ultraviolet light; looser brushwork than was the case with Lindauer's work; an absence of pencil underdrawing, which would be visible under infrared light; and use of natural ultramarine pigment. Hillary noted that the front of the painting had very little evidence of ageing – a lack of mechanical cracks and soiling – which was 'unusual for a painting on canvas that is around 100 years old'.

There was, then, compelling evidence that the painting was not by Lindauer, yet for well over a decade the fraud had gone undetected. With no other Lindauer paintings in the collections of Trust Waikato or the Waikato Museum with which it could be compared, no one had questioned its authenticity. And, as is the case with many regional museums, the staff did not have the specialist knowledge or necessary equipment to examine the painting in detail.

IN A CASE LIKE THIS there are challenges around terminology. When the deception was uncovered, many media reports used the word 'forgery' – that is, a work made with the deliberate intention of deceiving a would-be buyer into thinking it was the real thing. 'Fake' might be seen as a more appropriate term: the painting is almost certainly not by Lindauer yet it is an attempt to emulate the painter's style. For all we know, it could originally have been made as a copy by someone who wanted it for their own private viewing. However, the painting was signed G Lindauer and in recent times was marketed and sold as a Lindauer, which is fraudulent.

A third option would be to call it a copy, but it is not a direct copy of any known portrait. It has fundamental differences, such as the style and shape of the greenstone mere and cloak, from the only other known portrait of the sitter, thc one in the Auckland Art Gallery collection. It is possible the artist copied this and made a few changes and additions of his or her own. I have chosen to refer to the work as a fake, because technically that is what it is. However, if we knew for certain that the original maker had intended to sell it as a genuine work by Lindauer, and therefore to deceive the buyer, it would be a forgery.

AS THE STORY UNFOLDED so did details of the painting's provenance. It had apparently been acquired in Scotland during the 1990s by a New Zealander, who had then brought it to New Zealand. Webb's auction house in Auckland had subsequently offered the work for sale on two occasions: September 1997 and June 1998. Both times the estimated price range was put at $55,000 to $75,000 and the painting was passed in. It may have been on-sold later or retained by the owner. In 2001 it turned up in the catalogue of another Auckland art auction house, the International Art Centre, where it was bought by Trust Waikato.

It seemed extraordinary that the trust had relied on only one opinion – that of Stuart Stubbs – before spending a large sum of public money on the work. Both an expert such as Roger Blackley and a skilled conservator could have been brought in to examine the work and assess its authenticity. And a quick bit of research would have revealed that the painting had been offered at Webb's three years earlier for $55,000 to $75,000. Why was it on sale at another auction house only three years later with an estimated value of $140,000 to $160,000 when the value of Lindauer works had not doubled in that time? For Trust Waikato, the inescapable conclusion that the painting was not an authentic Lindauer meant its value had plummeted. Its fair-value market insurance valuation was now a mere $5,000.

Faced with the accusation that the painting was a practically worthless fake, the International Art Centre's director Richard Thomson denied the company should bear any responsibility. 'Saying it is a fake is a very strong statement,' he told a *Waikato Times* reporter, Chris Gardner, 'and I'm not about to comment on that. 'The people you need to talk to are the people who've been hanging it for ten years – this is really not my business. We could ask a lot of questions about a lot of paintings.'

To date, the centre has not provided any evidence of authenticity to the trust or the museum.

WHAT WAS WAIKATO MUSEUM TO DO with the fake portrait? New Zealand does not have a law dictating the treatment of inauthentic works of art – unlike France, where such works must be destroyed. In February 2014 an Englishman, Martin Lang, was ordered by a French magistrate to burn a 1911 painting he owned called *Reclining Nude*. Lang had bought the painting for £100,000 in 1992, believing it to be by the famous Russian Jewish artist Marc Chagall, who lived and worked mostly in France until his death in 1985. Lang had enjoyed the painting for over two decades before his son presented it to the BBC television programme *Fake or Fortune* for authentication. It was sent to the Chagall Committee in Paris, which pronounced it a forgery.

Closer to home, an Australian lawsuit in 2010 saw the Victorian Supreme Court order the destruction of three works falsely attributed to two well-known artists, Charles Blackman and Robert Dickerson. The paintings, which had been fraudulently valued and offered for sale by Peter Gant, an art dealer, were described by the judge as 'deliberately contrived to mislead the unsuspecting public'. He ordered them returned to the artists for destruction. Asked by a reporter from *The Age* how he would destroy the fakes, eighty-six-year-old Dickerson suggested he would rip them up with his bare hands.

The same fate may befall two more paintings sold by Peter Gant and a third one offered for sale by him. In December 2007 Andrew Pridham, chairman of the Australian rules football club Sydney Swans, purchased from Gant, via an art consultant, a large painting by one of Australia's best-loved artists, Brett Whiteley. *Big Blue Lavender Bay* – the title refers to the view from the late artist's home in Sydney – cost Pridham AU$2.5 million. When

Whiteley's widow Wendy Whiteley visited Pridham's house in April 2008 to view the painting she was suspicious: it didn't feel right.

It was not the first Brett Whiteley painting to not feel right. One purchased from Gant the previous year for AU$1.1 million had also come under suspicion. A third had been offered for sale by Gant at just under a million dollars. It was not long before both Gant and the suspected forger, a respected Melbourne art conservator named Mohamed Aman Siddique, were arrested and charged with fraud. The police had been tipped off by one of Siddique's employees who had peered over a partition and seen fake artworks in progress. Gant had purchased a genuine Whiteley painting in order to have Siddique copy the techniques. In May 2016, after a five-week trial, both men were found guilty.

THERE WAS TO BE NO DESTRUCTION of Trust Waikato's fake Lindauer. In 2013 the trust decided to keep it on the grounds that its intrinsic worth to local iwi as a portrait of an ancestor was too important to de-accession it. And what would have become of the work if it were to be de-accessioned but not destroyed? Ethically the trust could not sell it: even if it was clearly labelled as not being painted by Lindauer, it could still find its way back on to the open market as a genuine work.

Staff at Waikato Museum were now faced with the task of deciding on a new label for the painting. The museum's online catalogue first noted opaquely that the work was 'attributed to Gottfried Lindauer original'. A more apt description might have been 'in the manner of Lindauer' or 'in the style of Lindauer'. Today the catalogue simply refers to it as a copy, 'Artist, Unknown'.

Internationally, there is a trend among some institutions to be more actively transparent about changes to a work's authenticity or provenance. A 2,500-year-old bowl, the Euphronios Krater, which was acquired by New York's Metropolitan Museum of Art in 1971, was subsequently discovered to have been looted from an Etruscan tomb and sold illegally. In 2006 the krater and several other artifacts were officially repatriated to Italy. At Rome's Villa Giulia, which now houses it, a label spells out its criminal background.

At the J. Paul Getty Museum in Los Angeles doubt continues over the authenticity of a larger-than-life Greek marble sculpture of a nude youth, colloquially known as the Getty Kouros. Acquired in 1985, the work cost US$9.5 million. Even before the purchase some experts noticed stylistic inconsistencies, such as the hair and feet being fashioned in the styles of different time periods. However, the museum was reassured when scientific analysis of the statue's surface revealed that the magnesium component of the dolomitic marble – calcium magnesium carbonate – had leached out, a process it was thought could have occurred only naturally and over a period of centuries.

Subsequent research showed that magnesium could, in fact, be removed artificially from dolomitic marble, and in 1990 an antiquities dealer unearthed a torso similar to the Getty Kouros, which was believed to have been fabricated in a Rome workshop in the early 1980s. To signal the doubt about the authenticity of the sculpture, the label now reads, 'Greek, about 530 B.C., or modern forgery'.

BY 2013 MANY IN THE NEW ZEALAND ART WORLD were well aware of the existence of fake Lindauers. Astonishingly, however, in April that year the Alexander Turnbull Library purchased for $75,900 a portrait of a Māori man, Haoni or Hamiora Maioha, supposedly by Lindauer, after being warned by Roger Blackley that the work was probably not genuine. The auction catalogue noted that the work was most likely a private commission and gave its provenance as having come from a private Hawke's Bay collection.

Blackley's suspicions were confirmed in 2015 when Sarah Hillary, carrying out research for a book on Lindauer, examined the painting and discovered the presence of titanium dioxide-based pigment, a substance not commonly available in Lindauer's time. Other telltale signs were a lack of craquelure, fine cracks, on the surface of the painting, and unevenness in the way the canvas was stretched.

The Alexander Turnbull Library had had a week's period of grace after the auction to carry out further due diligence, and could have had the painting analysed and tested. Instead, confident with the view of its in-house authority that it was genuine, it had squandered public money on a fraudulent work.

IT IS INTERESTING TO NOTE that whereas the provenance of the Trust Waikato 'Lindauer' remains largely a mystery, Auckland Art Gallery's portrait of Kewene Te Haho has a very clear line. It is known the painting was sold by Lindauer to Henry Partridge, an Auckland businessman who was one of the artist's earliest and most dedicated clients. Partridge would amass more than seventy paintings by Lindauer and even name one of his daughters Myra Lindauer. In 1915 he donated all his Lindauer works, including the portrait of Kewene Te Haho, to the people of Auckland, conditional on the city raising by subscription the sum of £10,000, to be donated to the Belgian Refugee Fund. Germany had invaded Belgium on August 4, 1914 and within weeks 600,000 Belgians had fled to Holland and France. The Lindauer paintings gifted by Henry Partridge remain in the gallery's collection to this day.

NINE

Pania of the Reef

FROM ITS INSTALLATION IN 1954, the life-size bronze sculpture *Pania of the Reef* was an intrinsic and much-loved part of the city of Napier's waterfront. For some it was as important to Napier as Edvard Eriksen's bronze statue *The Little Mermaid* was to Copenhagen. For over fifty years Pania had led a largely uneventful life: apart from being once inexplicably shot in the head and subsequently repaired, she had sat calmly on her granite plinth. Then, on October 26, 2005, she was wrenched from the plinth and whisked away.

In Māori legend, Pania was a beautiful young woman who left her sea people to marry Karitoki, a chief who lived at what is today Sturm's Gully near Napier's Bluff Hill. Every day after she had visited Karitoki her people would call her back to the sea. One day, when she resisted, they dragged her down deep into the ocean, where she remains to this day as Pania Reef.

In 1951 a search was undertaken to find a model for Napier's newest public sculpture, which had been commissioned by a local group, the Thirty Thousand Club. A thirteen-year-old girl, Mei

Robin, a student at Hukarere Māori Girls' College, was selected and the sculpture was made in Carrara, Italy, based on photographs. Fearing Mei's piupiu could end up looking like a Hawaiian grass skirt, the commissioners sent an actual piupiu to Italy for the sculptor to work from, together with detailed drawings of the tiki that was to hang around her neck. The sculpture was unveiled in 1954 by the prime minister, Sidney Holland.

ON THE MORNING OF OCTOBER 27, 2005 Napier City Council staff were informed that *Pania* had disappeared. It was clear the culprits had given some thought to how to remove the life-size sculpture, which weighed about seventy kilograms. Brute force would have been required as the bolts attaching the sculpture to the granite plinth had been torn off. An escape vehicle would also have been needed.

There was an outpouring of public rage and grief, and floral tributes amassed on the empty plinth. There was speculation that the thieves had been inspired by a similar incident three weeks earlier, when *Long Horizon*, a sculpture by Paul Dibble, one of New Zealand's foremost sculptors, and valued at $250,000, had been taken at night from the grounds of a restaurant at Waikanae Beach, north of Wellington. This sculpture had weighed more than a tonne; the thieves had brought special equipment with them to remove the bolts that held the two pieces of the sculpture together, and those that attached it to its concrete base.

A reward of $10,000 for the sculpture's return had been paid after a man sent a local newspaper a video showing he had the work. Later Brenden John Marshall turned himself into the police and was charged with stealing the sculpture and blackmailing the owners: he had told them he would destroy the work and sell the bronze if the ransom were not paid. Sentenced to 300 hours of community service, he later appealed on the grounds that he was just the middleman and had received only $2,000 of the reward. The conviction was upheld. The thieves have never been caught.

NAPIER'S LOCAL MEMBER OF PARLIAMENT, Russell Fairbrother, declared he would speak to the mayor and police about raising funds to offer as a ransom for *Pania*'s safe return. The following day, presumably having thought better of it, he retracted the statement and suggested funds should instead be raised to offer a reward for information.

This is a problematic area: offering rewards and paying ransoms can have the perverse effect of both encouraging art theft and increasing the cost of insuring art. *Art Crime* author John Conklin has pointed to a paradox: if collectors didn't insure their artworks, insurance companies, who have to pay out for their loss, wouldn't offer rewards – and it's the prospect of a reward that can encourage a thief.

In New Zealand rewards have rarely been offered for the return of stolen artworks. There was an exception in August 2007 when *Ulysses*, a painting by artist Ralph Hotere with an asking price of $19,500, was stolen from a Queenstown dealer gallery in broad daylight; at the time the gallery owner was out the back answering the phone. A $5,000 reward was offered but the painting has never been found.

Rewards, even when offered, are not always paid out. When precious items that included a Goldie painting and a valuable Bible were stolen from the University of Auckland during a holiday break, a reward of $20,000 was offered by the insurers. The university received information that the items would be returned without the need for a reward payment if the culprits were not prosecuted. Raewyn Dalziel, then deputy vice chancellor, later recalled: 'As the Goldie and the Bible were valuable donated items we were anxious to have them back and agreed.'

Eight days after *Pania of the Reef* was stolen, police officers carrying out a routine search at a property for evidence of cannabis cultivation had a lucky break. In a shed they found the sculpture, almost unharmed. Three people, Che Te Kooti Dion Rogan, his wife Shiralee Valerie Rogan, and Charles Nukunuku, were charged with theft. The charge against the Rogans was later changed to a lesser one of receiving stolen property. Twenty-five-year-old Nukunuku, a debt collector, pleaded guilty and was sentenced to twelve months' imprisonment.

Through his lawyer, Amanda Courtney, Nukunuku appealed the sentence on the grounds that it was too harsh. A long-time advocate for restorative justice, Pat Magill, also slammed the sentence, maintaining that Nukunuku had spent time in prison in the past and there was nothing to be served by sending him there again. The presiding judge, Tony Adeane, did not agree. The theft, he said, had clearly been planned, not a spur-of-the-moment decision.

LIKE MANY OF THOSE WHO STEAL bronze sculptures, Nukunuku and his two helpers had undoubtedly hoped to make money from their crime but their chances were limited. Given the significance of the sculpture it would have been incredibly difficult not only to sell it but to even have it melted down for the bronze. And if they had succeeded in having it melted down, the gain would have been small. In 2005 a two-tonne sculpture, *Vanitas*, worth £3 million was stolen from the Henry Moore Foundation Gardens in Hertfordshire, England, by three men using a Mercedes truck and a crane. Police later received information that the huge bronze had been cut up for scrap, and shipped to China via Rotterdam in The Netherlands. The thieves were estimated to have received no more than £1,500.

Although the foundation vowed to ramp up its security, in July 2012 another Henry Moore sculpture, *Sundial*, was stolen from the gardens. A few days later the two thieves returned and helped themselves to the plinth on which the sculpture had sat. They sold the sculpture and plinth to a scrap-metal dealer, receiving £228 for their efforts.

By a stroke of luck the scrap-metal dealer saw a story about the theft on the BBC's *Crimewatch* programme. He alerted police, and the sculpture, valued at £500,000, was returned to the gardens. The thieves, aged nineteen and twenty-two, each received a jail sentence of twelve months.

The ripples were felt in New Zealand. London's *Independent* newspaper reported that a twenty-four-hour guard had been placed on a large Henry Moore sculpture, *Inner Form*, in Wellington's Botanic Garden after a tip-off that it was about to be stolen. The sculpture, said to be worth three million pounds, had been donated to the city by a construction company in 1988 as part of an arts bonus scheme whereby developers could increase the height of buildings in the CBD in exchange for donating public artworks. *Inner Form* had originally been sited on a small inner-city park, where it had been repeatedly vandalised.

Nothing came of the threat but perhaps the concern was

justified. In recent years there has been a spate of robberies of bronze sculptures from both public and domestic collections in New Zealand. In 2013 Friends of Auckland's Botanic Gardens raised funds to purchase *Tuna*, a bronze by a prominent sculptor, Bing Dawe. *Tuna* is Māori for eel, and the striking two-metre tall sculpture depicted a swimming long-fin eel. On July 20, 2014 thieves with a hacksaw cut through the bolts anchoring the work, which weighed ninety kilograms, and made off with it from its site in the threatened native plants section of the gardens.

Staff made it their business to immediately contact scrap-metal dealers in the region and within twenty-four hours police had received a call from Metalman, a dealer who had been offered the work. The two thieves were swiftly caught and charged. *Tuna* was valued at $30,000. If the men had got away with their crime, they would have made at most $360.

In an effort to increase the weight of the hollow sculpture, and therefore sell it for more, the men had sawn off the tail and fins to pour water inside. The extensive damage was repaired, and at the artist's request *Tuna* was returned to its original position in the gardens. The bronze pin running through the work was replaced with one of stainless steel: bronze has the propensity to snap rather than bend, so making it easier for the wannabe thief. The circular plates that hold the sculpture to the pedestal are now also stainless steel.

PUBLIC SCULPTURES ARE NOT the only ones targeted. In 2014 a couple living in the seaside town of Mount Maunganui were on holiday when they got an email from a neighbour. Attached were images of their beloved bronze sculpture *From Memory*, by a noted sculptor, Terry Stringer. The large work was in a terrible state. Thieves had attempted to wrest it out of the ground but been thwarted by its metre-long stainless steel rods. In the process they had bent the rods ninety degrees and the sculpture was now flattened. This had been a particularly bold crime: the house was in a built-up area and the garden in which the sculpture stood faced directly on to a public green space. The culprits were never found.

Just a few months earlier another Terry Stringer sculpture had been stolen from a public place in Auckland. Fearing copycat crimes, neither the owner nor the insurers had made the theft public, and Stringer had quickly replaced the sculpture with another the same.

Opportunist art thieves are getting ever more audacious. In 2014 another large work by Paul Dibble was stolen from outside an art gallery in Chews Lane, a busy walkway in downtown Wellington. *Soft Geometric Pacific Comb*, which was being sold by Page Blackie Gallery on behalf of the estate of its deceased owner, weighed 120 kilograms. It was located across the road from the city's central police station and protected at night by two security grills. These had not been tampered with. It's possible they had not been locked one night, or the work had been stolen by someone with a swipe card and keys to the grills.

Although the work went missing at the end of February, the loss was not made public until March 18 to give the police time to investigate without alerting the culprits. When this failed, appeals were made for its return. The police stressed that as a work of art it had an estimated value of $65,000 but its worth in scrap metal was only a few hundred dollars. The gallery, for its part, decided against offering a reward on the grounds that it would set a precedent and could encourage copycat crimes. *Soft Geometric Pacific Comb* has never been recovered.

NOT ONLY ARE PUBLIC SCULPTURES attractive to thieves, they are also popular with vandals. *Little Bull*, a bronze sculpture by Molly Macalister, chosen in 1967 for Hamilton Gardens after a public competition, had been installed only a month before it was daubed with green, red and white paint, with a touch of gold on each horn. In 2011 a stone sculpture by a Canterbury artist, Russell Clark, which featured a boy riding Opo, a famous dolphin that had frequented local waters in the summer of 1955/56 until dying accidentally or being murdered, was attacked on its beachfront site in the town of Opononi and the boy's head snapped off. The sculpture, created four years after Opo's death, had suffered earlier attacks. A businessman launched a fund to have the statue recast in bronze at a cost of $90,000, and in 2013 it was unveiled on the site of the original.

Two thousand and eleven also saw a much-loved bronze statue of Wellington's city father John Plimmer and his dog Fritz, which had stood at the entrance to a downtown lane since 1966, tagged with white and orange spray paint. This was not the duo's first indignity. In 1998 and again in 2000 vandals had cut off Fritz's tail. Today the tail has a concealed steel rod to prevent future amputations.

Fortunately, vandalised sculptures can often be cleaned or fixed, unlike those that are stolen and never seen again. Ironically the noisy media attention given an act of vandalism or theft can also alert citizens to the presence of a public artwork they hadn't previously known about. A work can become famous for all the wrong reasons.

THE MOTIVE FOR THE THEFT of *Pania of the Reef* was never clear: all Nukunuku could offer by way of an explanation was that the statue was a good luck charm. Clearly, his luck ran out when he was convicted and sentenced. On November 16, less than a month after it had disappeared in the night, *Pania of the Reef* was restored to her former glory on Napier's Marine Parade. Over a thousand people welcomed her home; Mei, the original model for the sculpture, was given the honour of unveiling her.

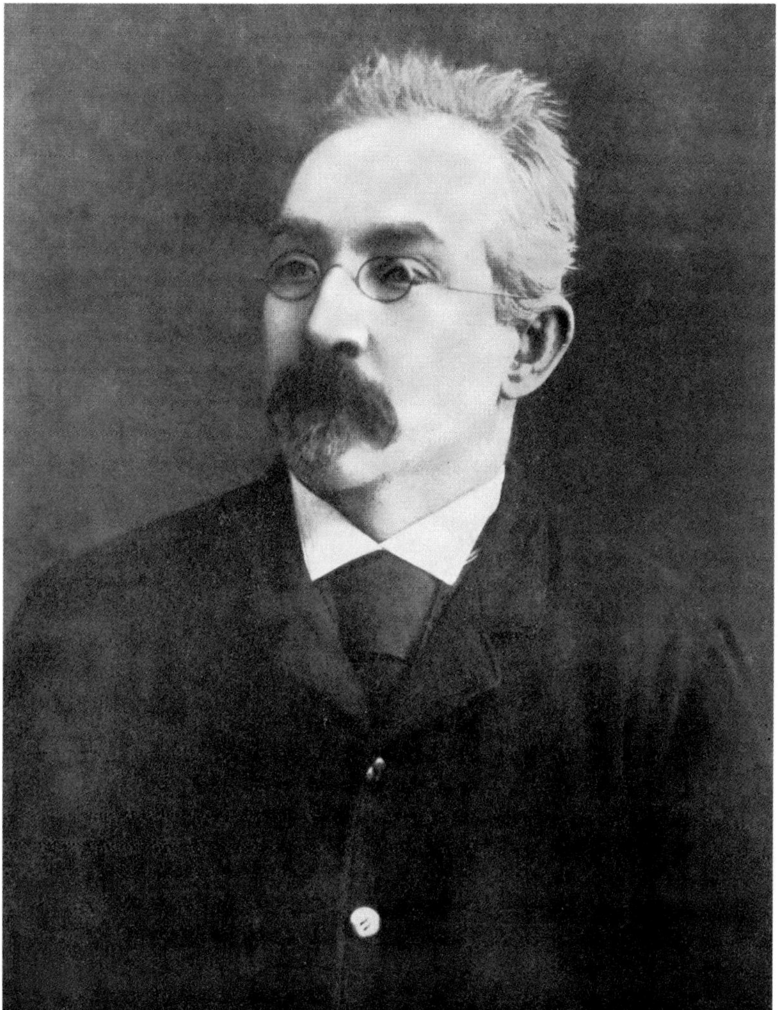

Gottfried Lindauer, who became a noted painter of Māori portraits, trained in art at a Viennese academy and arrived in New Zealand in 1874. Today many of his portraits are cherished by descendants of the subjects and are seen as valuable historical records. *Alexander Turnbull Library PUBL-0092-001*

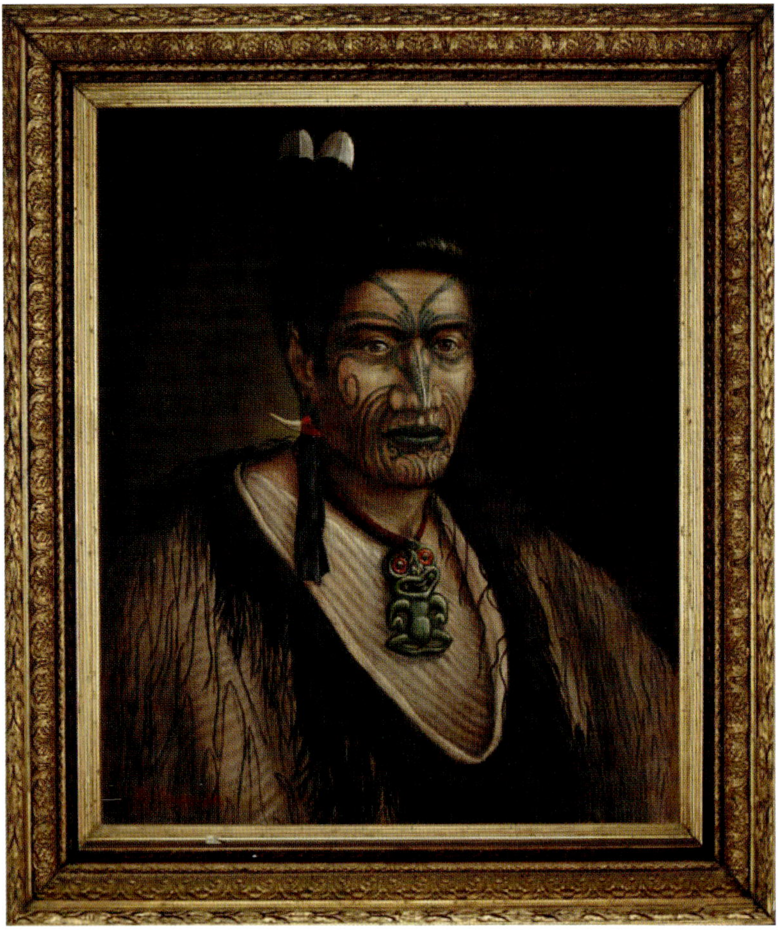

This well-executed portrait of a Māori man named as Hoani or Hamiora Maioha, signed G. Lindauer, was deemed a fake by a Lindauer expert but purchased nonetheless by Alexander Turnbull Library for $75,900 on the advice of its in-house staff in 2013. By this time many in the art world were well aware of the existence of fake Lindauers. The painting contained titanium dioxide-based pigment, a substance not commonly available in Lindauer's time. Other telltale signs were a lack of fine cracks on the surface and unevenness in the way the canvas was stretched.

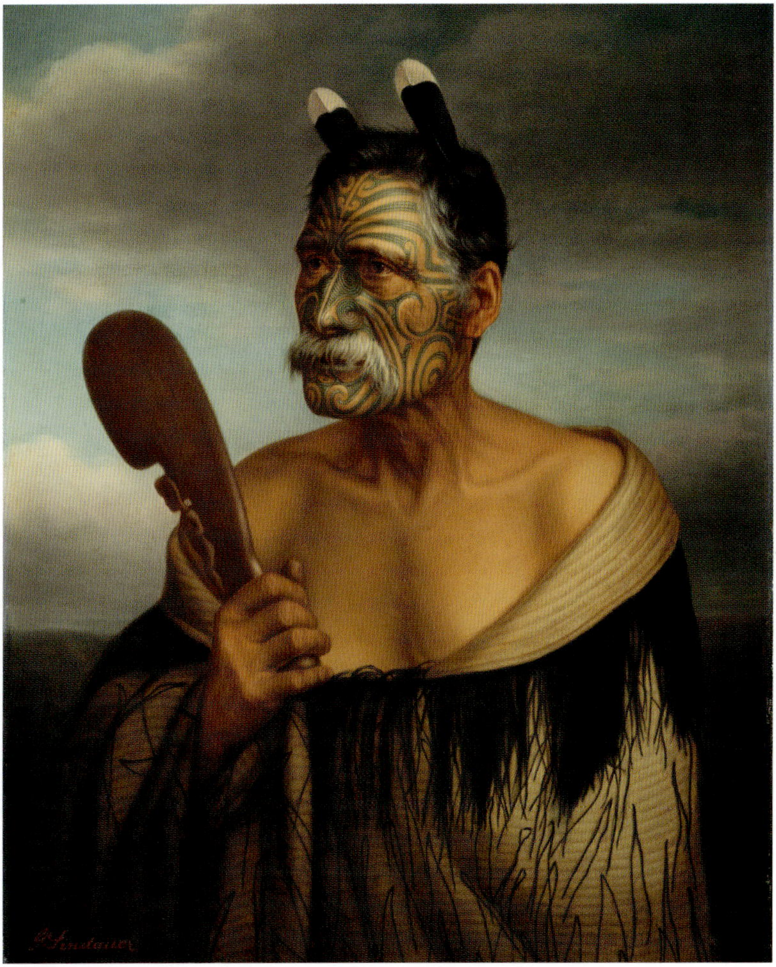

A genuine Lindauer painting – of Māori elder Kewene Te Haho – held by Auckland Art Gallery Toi o Tāmaki; in 1902 it was acknowledged by his son, Ratapu Kewene, to be a portrait of his father. The painting has a clear provenance, having been donated to the city of Auckland by Henry Partridge, one of the artist's most avid collectors of the day.

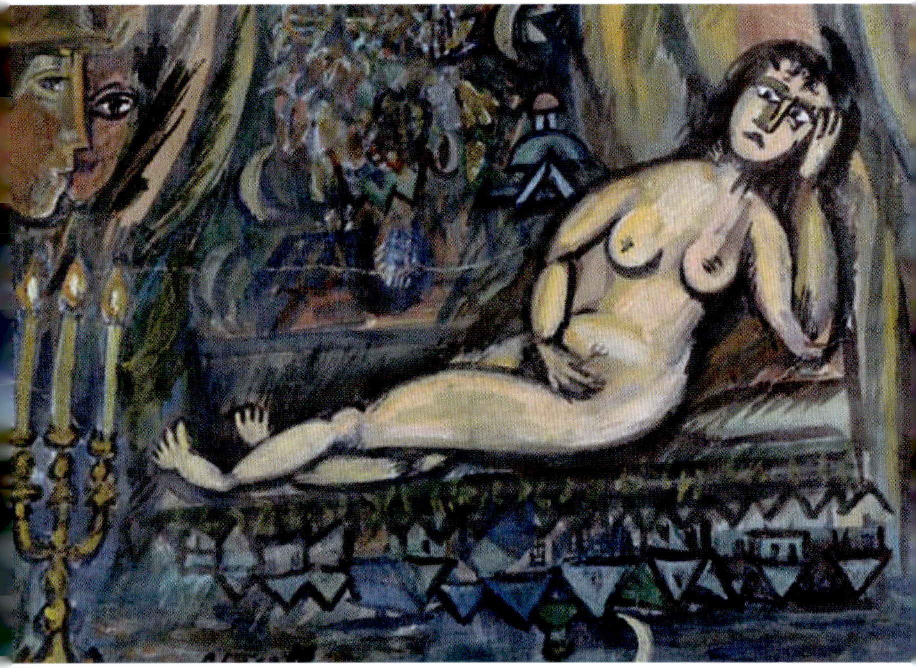

When paintings are found to be forgeries, some countries, France among them, require their destruction. This was the fate of this painting, *Reclining Nude*, after it was pronounced inauthentic by the Chagall Committee in Paris. It had been bought by an Englishman for £100,000 in 1992 as a work by the famous Russian Jewish artist, who lived and worked mostly in France.

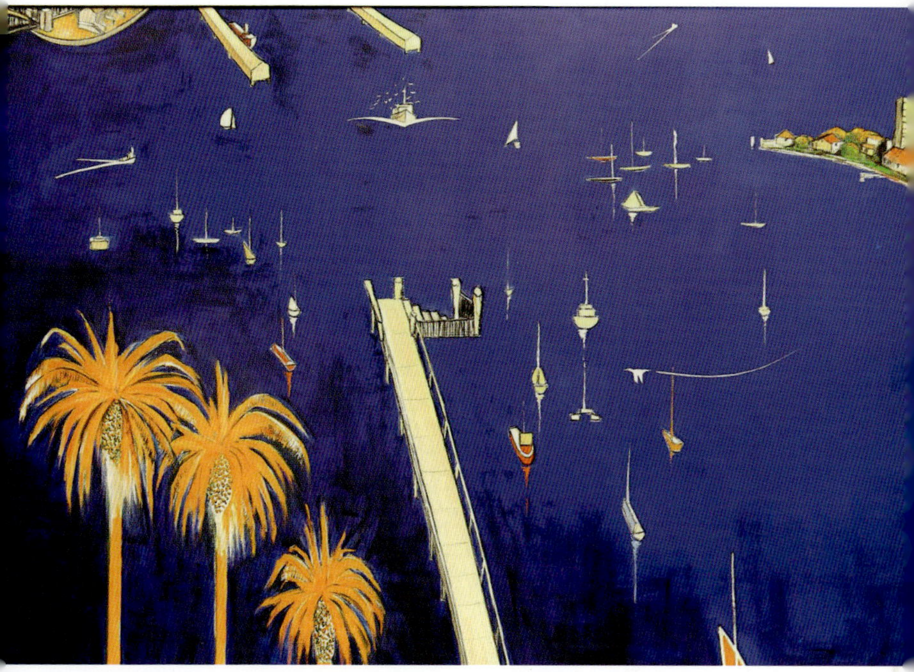

In a case that rocked Australia in 2016, a leading art conservator, Mohamed Siddique, and art dealer Peter Gant were found guilty of producing and selling fake paintings, purporting they were by the renowned artist Brett Whiteley. This one, titled *Big Blue Lavender Bay*, was sold for AU$2.5 million and the other for $1.1. million. The fraud came to light when Whiteley's widow, Wendy Whiteley, visited the owner of *Big Blue Lavender Bay* for a viewing; she pronounced his expensive acquisition a fake.

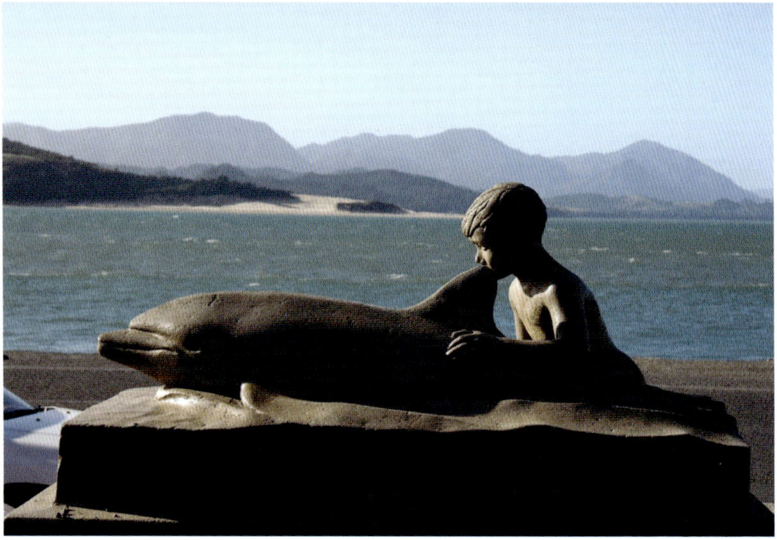

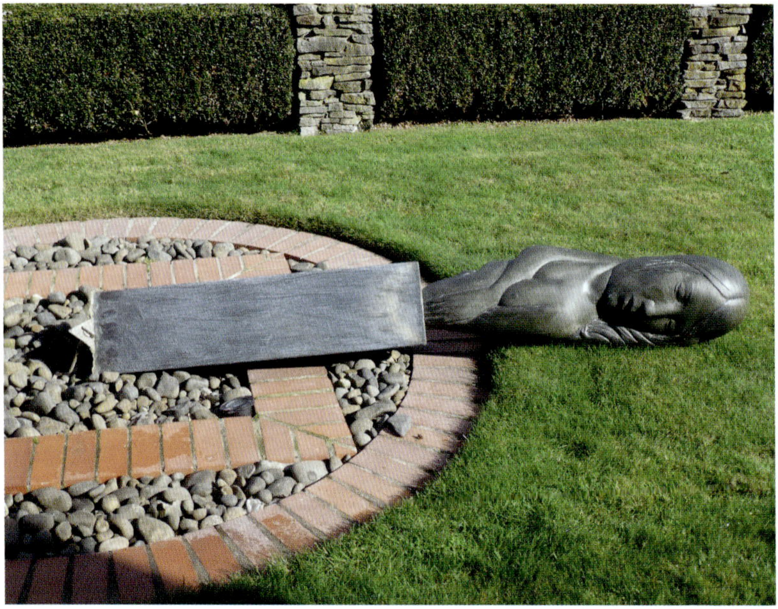

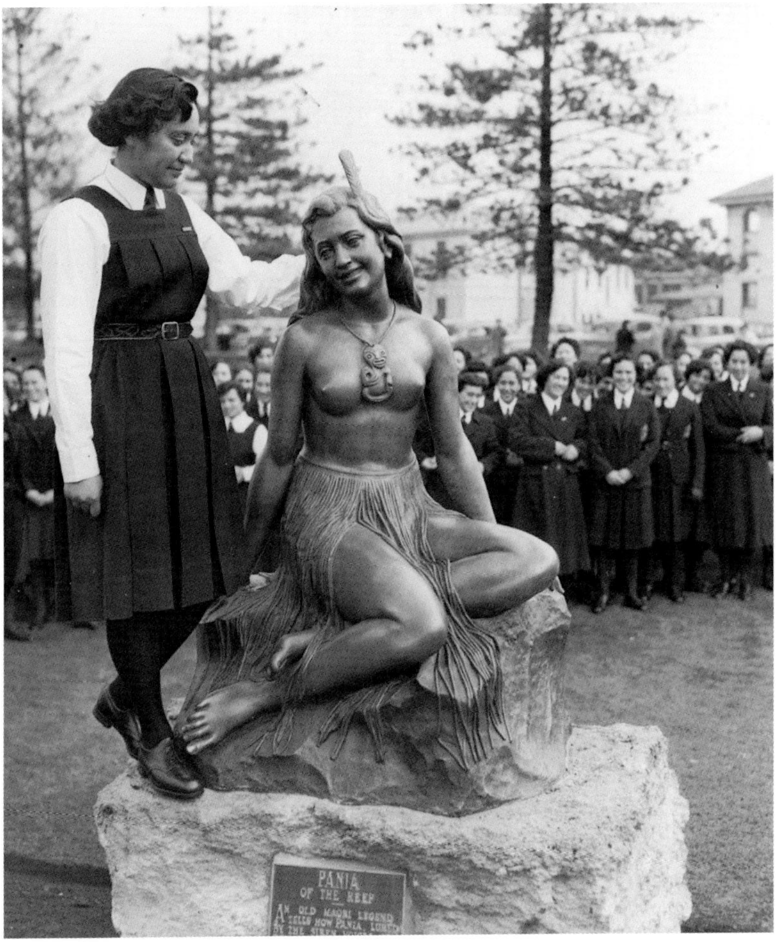

LEFT, ABOVE A stone statue of Opo the dolphin on the Opononi beachfront in 2010. The following year it was attacked and the boy's head snapped off. *Photographer Richard Joseph*

LEFT, BELOW *From Memory,* this bronze sculpture by Terry Stringer, was vandalised in the garden of its owners, which overlooked a public green space. The thieves' efforts to abscond with the work were thwarted by the metre-long stainless steel rods holding it in the ground. *Graeme and Susan Horsley Collection*

ABOVE Schoolgirl Mei Irihapiti Robin, the model for *Pania of the Reef,* poses with the bronze sculpture at its unveiling in Napier in June 1954. The work was stolen in 2005. Police came upon it serendipitously while doing a routine search of a property for cannabis cultivation: the sculpture was in a shed.
Alexander Turnbull Library PACoII-6585-88

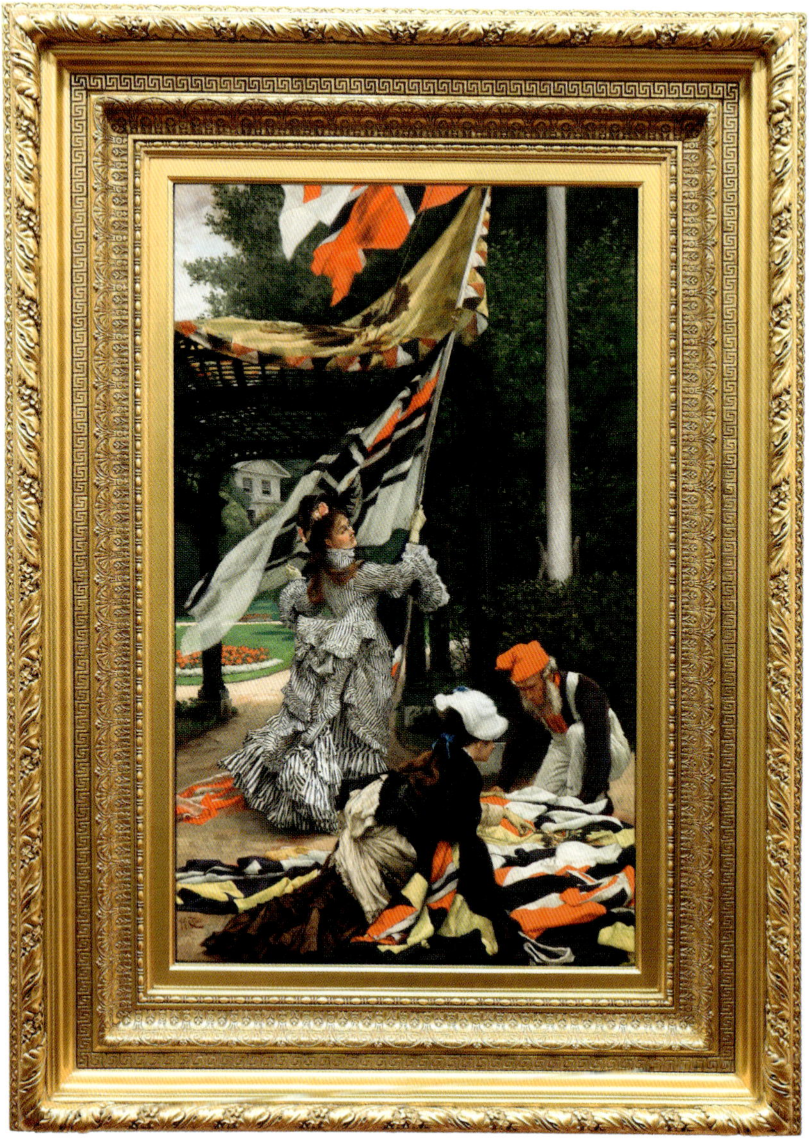

Still on Top, a painting by Jacques Joseph (James) Tissot in the collection of Auckland Art Gallery Toi o Tāmaki. In August 1998, in a premeditated theft, one of New Zealand's leading career criminals raced into the gallery, wrested the $2 million painting from the wall, ripped it from its frame, ran out the door with it, and departed on his motorbike. *Auckland Art Gallery Toi o Tāmaki*

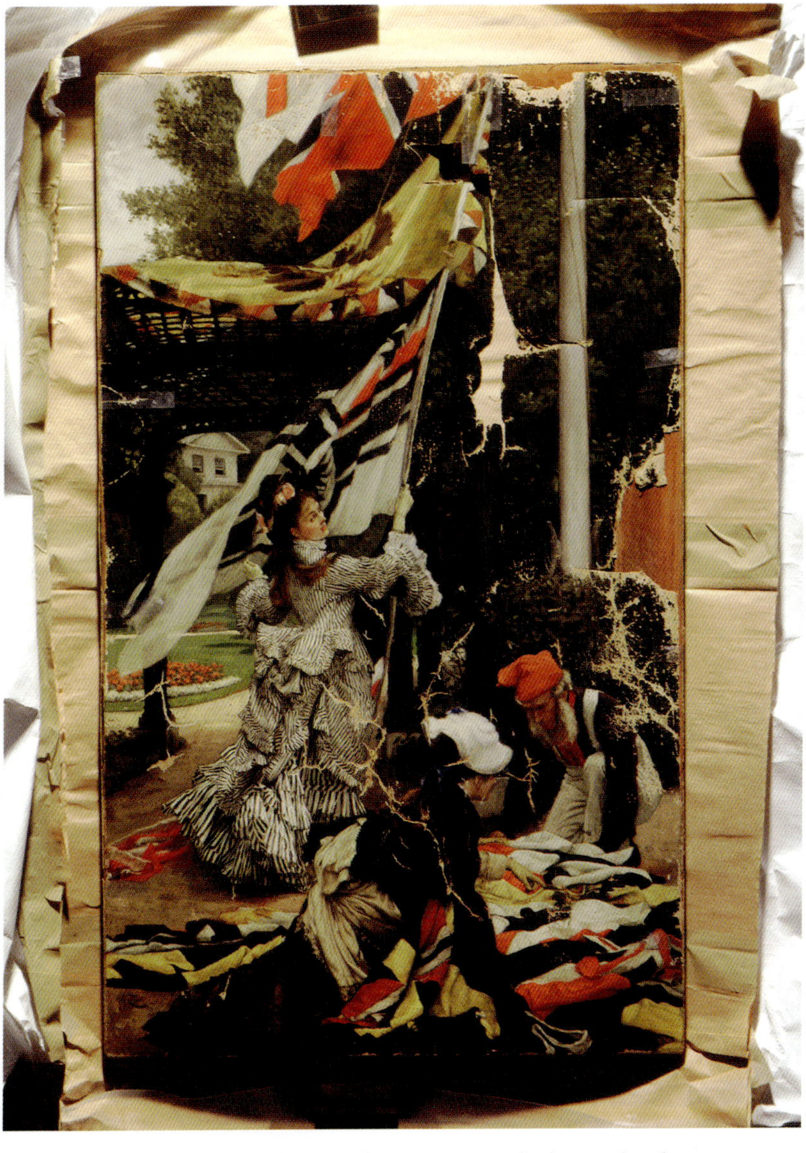

When the painting was discovered it was extensively damaged and required costly restoration. *Auckland Art Gallery Toi o Tāmaki*

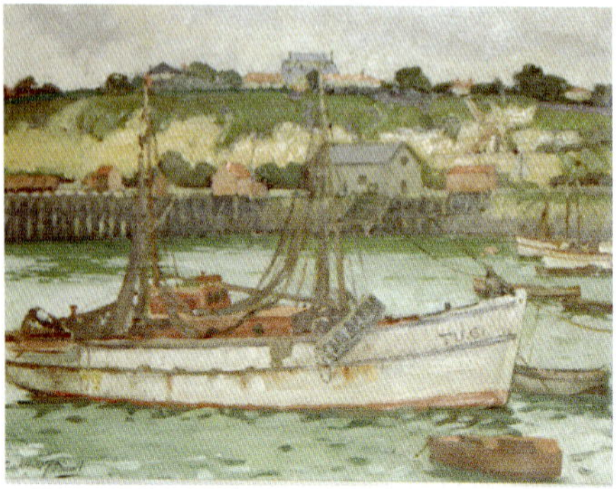

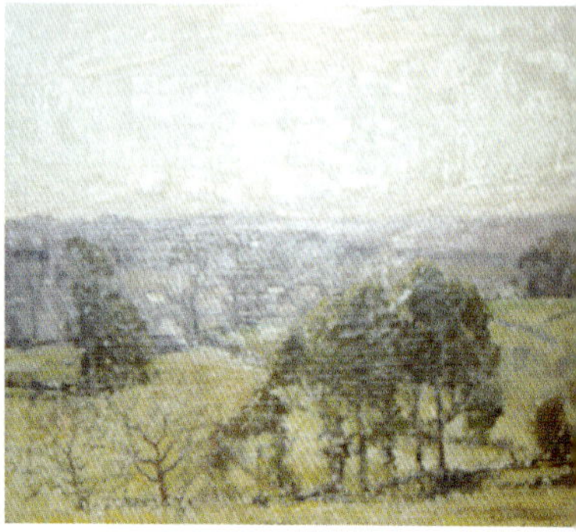

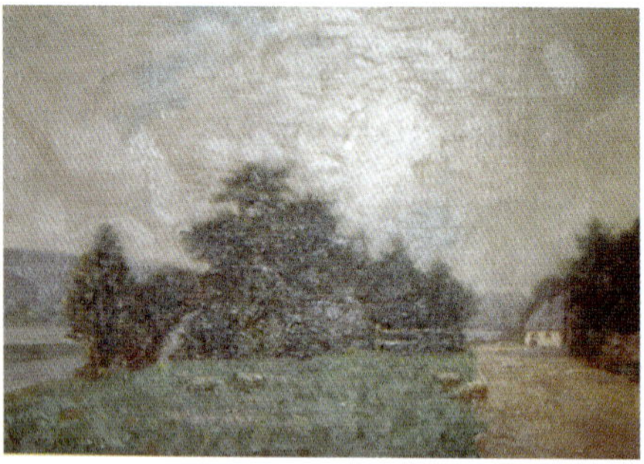

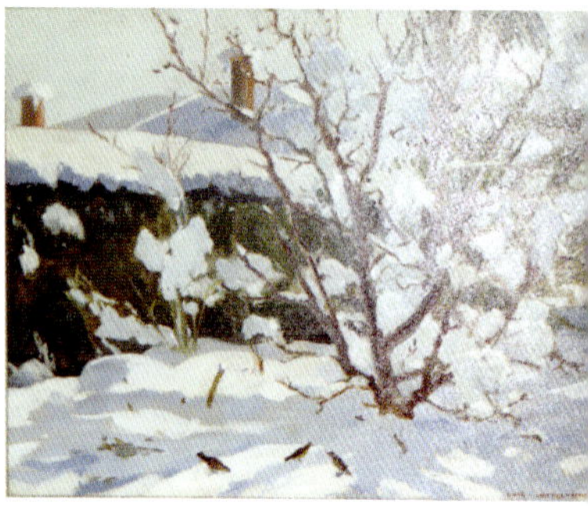

ABOVE, TOP *Fishing Boats Timaru* by Archibald Frank Nicoll, 1932.
ABOVE *Scottish Landscape with Sheep* by William Menzies Gibb, c. 1910.
RIGHT, TOP *Australian Landscape* by Robert H. Johnson, c. 1948.
RIGHT, BELOW *Snowstorm* by Rata Lovell-Smith, 1945.
All photographs Elizabeth Wearn Collection

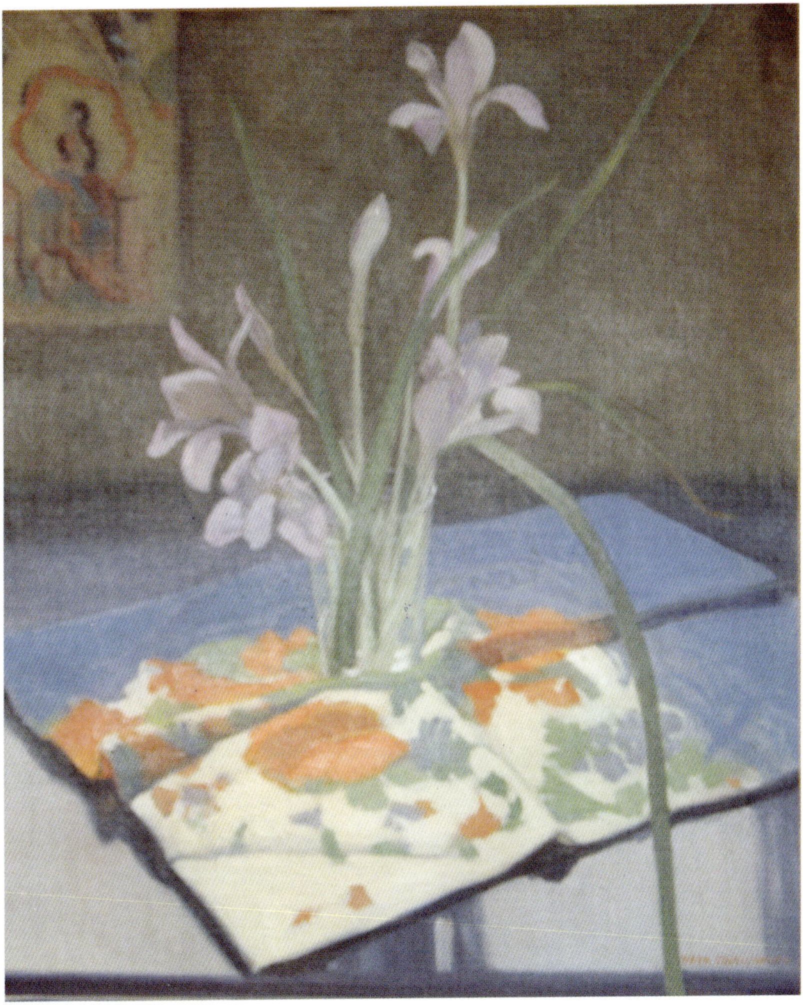

Still Life with Irises by Rata Lovell-Smith, 1950. All five paintings on these pages were stolen from a home in the Auckland suburb of Remuera when the owner was out. They have never been found. These faded photographs are the only evidence they ever existed. *Elizabeth Wearn Collection*

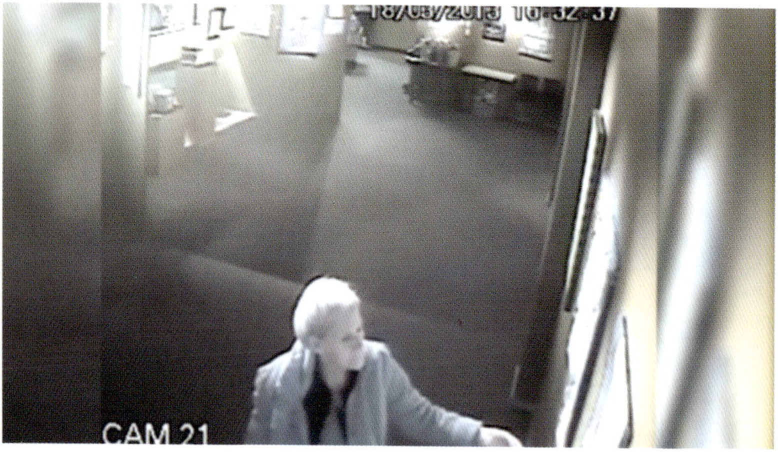

ABOVE In a brazen theft a British tourist in her mid seventies walked into a gallery in the South Island town of Arrowtown, checked hanging devices on several works, lifted a valuable quilt by a local artist off the wall and stuffed it in her bag. Her movements were filmed on close-circuit television linked directly to the local police station and she was arrested next day. *New Zealand Police*

BELOW *Phoenix Rising*, a two-metre-tall stainless steel sculpture by artist Keith Simpson,was recovered from a property in a village in the central North Island by police in March 2014, after being spotted in an online real estate advertisement. It had been stolen ten years before from outside a community library in Auckland. *Lane Demchy photograph*

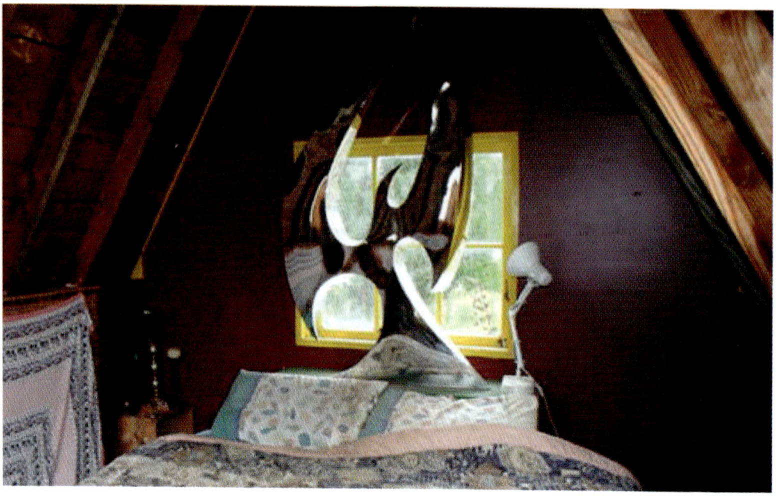

TEN

For love of Elena

IT WAS AUGUST 1998 AND RICARDO SANND was keen to make his rented property at Waikaretu, a small rural settlement, homelier for the impending arrival of his Uzbekistani wife, Elena Romanov.[23] The couple had recently married in Singapore after a long-distance courtship. Using the proceeds of armed robberies he had carried out in and around Auckland and Northland, Sannd had purchased expensive kitchenware and appliances,[24] but the pièce de résistance was to be a painting – a beautiful Victorian work called *Still on Top* by French artist Jacques Joseph Tissot.

On the morning of August 9 Sannd got on his Honda CBR 1100XX Super Blackbird motorbike and rode 100 kilometres to Auckland. At 11.45 a.m., still wearing his motorbike helmet, he entered Auckland Art Gallery and headed for the Lower Wellesley Gallery, where the institution's most significant historical works were on display. After jabbing a security guard with a Winchester Defender single-barrel shotgun, he made straight for *Still on Top*. He knew exactly where the painting was: he had visited the gallery previously and calculated it to be sixty-three metres from the main entrance.

Using brute force, Sannd wrested the painting from the wall and flung it on the floor, breaking the glass. With the aid of a crowbar, he then ripped the canvas, still on its stretcher, from its heavy gilt frame and ran out the door. Strapping the painting on his back, he got on the Honda, fired the sawn-off shotgun over his head to ward off a gallery visitor who was in hot pursuit only four metres away, and took off. Within the space of three minutes and ten seconds, a valuable Tissot painting had been stolen and severely damaged by one of New Zealand's most notorious criminals.

JACQUES JOSEPH TISSOT, usually known by the anglicised name James, which he adopted as a young man, was born in Nantes in 1836. He pursued an artistic career from the age of twenty, becoming classically trained, and in his early twenties was accepted to exhibit at the Paris Salon. He was a contemporary of Édouard Manet, Edgar Degas and Berthe Morisot; his later style could be described as French Realist/Impressionist, although he refused to exhibit with the Impressionists.

Immediately after fighting for France on the side of the Communards during the Prussian siege of 1870 to 1871, Tissot fled to London and settled in a lavish house at 17 (now 44) Grove End Road, St John's Wood. Tissot's father was a draper and his mother a milliner, and he excelled at depicting textiles and clothing. He became financially successful, selling expensive paintings of elegant upper-class women to a keen market of well-heeled Londoners.

In many of Tissot's works, beautiful women languish on shipboard or are seen dancing. *Still on Top*, painted about two years after Tissot had settled in London, was unusual. Two young women are in a garden – in fact Tissot's own at 17 Grove End Road – engaged in raising flags with the assistance of an elderly male servant. Both women wear exquisitely detailed Victorian dresses, while the servant sports overalls and a Communard's cap, showing his defiance of the Versailles authorities who had surrendered France to Prussia.

At the top of the composition the British Ensign is just visible. It has been suggested that Tissot, in naming the painting, was indicating that Britain was superior to the European nations but this is far from clear. A companion piece, *Preparing for the Gala*, depicts the same scene with a slightly wider vista.

THE PAINTING, WHICH LEFT LONDON on SS *Ruahine* in December 1920 bound for New Zealand, has a fascinating provenance. Valued at £500, it had been gifted to Auckland Art Gallery by Lord Leverhulme, a British industrialist who had made a fortune manufacturing Sunlight Soap through his company, Lever Brothers. Leverhulme, who also had a brief political career, was a generous philanthropist and a passionate art collector who would acquire 20,000 artworks in his lifetime. Less admirably, from 1911 he set up palm oil plantations in the Belgian Congo that ruthlessly exploited workers and were the subject of widespread protest.

It is probable that Leverhulme was the first owner of the painting, which was acquired for Auckland through the services of Thomson Wilson Leys, the editor of the *Auckland Star*. Leys was a patron of the arts and sat on the gallery's board. Leverhulme also gifted several works by Edward Burne-Jones to the gallery, and six, including *A Greek Water Carrier in Egypt* by William Blake Richmond, to the Sarjeant Gallery Te Whare o Rehua Whanganui. A good example of Tissot's work, *Still on Top* had been borrowed for international exhibitions in the United States in 1968 and Japan in 1988.

THE MEDIA REPORTED THAT *Still on Top* had a value of two million dollars, and Auckland police were quick to react to its theft. As an armed robbery, it had high priority. New Zealand Customs was alerted in case the perpetrator tried to leave New Zealand with the painting, and Interpol sent out a bulletin to stymie any attempt to sell it on the international market. The gallery's insurers, Royal and Sun Alliance, offered a $50,000 reward for information leading to its successful recovery.[25]

Soon after the heist the Auckland District Law Society received a Polaroid photograph of *Still on Top* and a ransom note for $500,000. The note was signed 'Chamelon'. It clearly came from Sannd. One of the conditions was that an Auckland lawyer, Megan Jenkins, was to handle the exchange of cash. Curiously, Jenkins did not know Sannd. The letter warned: 'Any police involvement would spell [sic] lots of blood you will not forget,' and noted: 'Any deviation/ violation of my conditions will ensure you never see the painting again – this is not negotiable.'

The police managed to track Sannd's telephone calls, perhaps after a tip-off from someone wanting the large reward, and on the morning of August 17 officers made their way to Waikaretu. Just after seven-thirty they searched Sannd's house and found the painting under his bed; at one stage he would claim he'd chanced upon it while vacuuming.

The find was bittersweet. The painting was in terrible condition. Police arranged for Auckland Art Gallery's principal conservator Sarah Hillary to meet them at Pukekohe Police Station so she could assess the damage. What greeted her was a badly severed painting stored in a sack.

When you work with a collection every day you become attached to the works and when one is damaged it becomes personal. A distressed Hillary later described what happened next: 'We brought [*Still on Top*] into the gallery and over the next few days the police would bring us little packages as they found them. It was so brittle but I was able to piece the bits together and use them.'

SANND WAS A CAREER CRIMINAL and the theft of the Tissot painting was just the latest in a catalogue of crimes. In 1984 he had taken part in New Zealand's biggest armed robbery when he and another man had robbed an Armourguard driver of $294,000 outside an Auckland supermarket. He had committed another armed robbery in Kerikeri in 1992 and three in and around Auckland in 1998. He had other convictions for theft, burglary and illegal use of weapons. His trial for stealing *Still on Top* – he was charged with armed robbery – lasted three weeks and for the latter part he dispensed with his lawyer and defended himself. He claimed he didn't need to steal the painting to on-sell it as he made enough money from benefit fraud. He also admitted to having raised $100,000 in quick cash by smuggling blue macaw parrots into New Zealand from South America.

Although Sannd was an experienced robber he had made some elementary mistakes. Ammunition he left on the gallery floor was a perfect match for ammunition police found at his home. He had made no attempt to conceal the details of the getaway vehicle. While following Sannd out of the gallery, an alert bystander, Richard Keuning, had recorded the number plate on the motorbike. The plate, 12TMZ, was found in the same room of Sannd's house as the Tissot. Police also found the typewriter that had been used to write the ransom note and a cartridge that matched the gun used during the robbery. Sannd was sentenced to just under seventeen years in prison.

The exact motive for the theft has never been fully established. There were a number of theories. The *New Zealand Herald* reported that early in 1998 Sannd had met a wealthy Hong Kong businessman at a Korean restaurant in suburban Auckland. The man, it was said, wanted a Tissot painting, in particular *Still on Top*, and was prepared to pay $800,000 for it. However, he had reneged on the deal when he heard the painting had been damaged.

Sannd himself would assert in an interview with the *Herald*'s Jonathan Milne in March 2012 that the theft had been commissioned but the story does not entirely stack up. The painting lay at his property for a week before the police found it. If it had been stolen to order it is likely he would have got rid of it quickly to avoid having it in his possession. And if a large amount of money was at stake, why had he not handled the painting carefully? By damaging it he had instantly devalued it, making it unsaleable without major conservation work. Lastly, why had he demanded a ransom if he already had a buyer?

STILL ON TOP WOULD HAVE A LONG ROAD to recovery. Restoring the painting would be Sarah Hillary's greatest challenge to date. Images of *Still on Top* dominated the media, both when the painting was lost and again after its return. The stunning work had captured the hearts of the public. There was enormous public pressure for the painting to be quickly restored and put back on display. At first it was anticipated that the restoration would take a year, but so great was the damage and so painstaking the work required that the project would occupy Hillary for nearly two years.

Before she could start, Hillary had to carry out extensive detective work. Although Tissot was a famous artist, little research had been undertaken on his technique and materials. Fortunately he had been very particular about both. Hillary and her team began the long and arduous process of restoration in February 1999. The final result was astounding. The next step was to reframe the work authentically as its frame had not been original. This was important since the artist would have chosen the frame himself, making it integral to the work. With advice from the Tate Gallery in London, where a Tissot painting still hangs in its original frame, a new $8,000 frame was fashioned in Australia from western red cedar and gilded with twenty-three-carat gold leaf. The total cost of restoration was $125,000, covered by the gallery's insurance.

On July 12, 2001 Auckland Art Gallery rehung *Still on Top*. It was accompanied by a display that described the painting's journey and restoration and showcased Tissot's work. The exhibition included *Waiting for the Train (Willesden Junction)*, a work painted around the same time as *Still on Top* and lent by the Dunedin Public Art Gallery, which had purchased it in 1921. The exhibition was hugely popular and ran for four months.

Not wanting to attract more and unwanted attention, galleries will usually try to deal with thefts in a low-key manner, even keeping the truth under wraps if possible, especially as a potential benefactor may be discouraged from donating a valuable work if it's known a gallery is vulnerable to theft. However, in the case of *Still on Top* the gallery had little choice: such a dramatic and violent crime was always going to to hit the headlines. Even after the trial, discussion continued to simmer in the media, including a complaint from Rape Crisis that the sentence received by Sannd was three times that handed down to rapists, and longer than many murderers served. Greater value, the organisation implied, was placed on artworks than on women.

LIKE MANY GALLERIES AND MUSEUMS, Auckland Art Gallery was no stranger to crime: it had been robbed three times in the past. Around two p.m. on July 21, 1966, perhaps when a security guard was distracted, someone had brazenly walked in and removed from its frame a small oil painting on wood. *Madonna and Child with Saint Sebastian* was the work of Paris Bordone, a sixteenth-century Venetian artist. It would later be described by art critic Mary Kisler, in her book *Angels and Aristocrats*, as showing 'the saint gazing in wonder and devotion at the proud mother and her bouncing naked child. He seems unaware that he is bound to a column, the arrow piercing his chest a minor inconvenience when compared to the vision that he sees before him.'

The painting had been sold at Christie's auction house in London on April 10, 1886 and had passed into the collection of the Coltart family in Liverpool. In 1957 it been brought to New Zealand by William Coltart, a farmer, when he immigrated. It was first shown in New Zealand in an exhibition, *Old Master Paintings from the Private and Public Collections of New Zealand*, in May 1959 and presented to the gallery the following year by the then owner, Norman Berridge Spencer, a businessman.

In an early lead, police had spent two hours fruitlessly searching a ship, *Tarawera*, after a tip-off. Then, four days after the disappearance of *Madonna and Child with Saint Sebastian*, the keeper of the gallery, Hamish Keith, received an anonymous phone call in which the caller revealed that the painting had been left at St Paul's, an historic Anglican church in Symonds Street. It had not been damaged, and three hours later was back on display.

Whether the thief had a particular penchant for Bordone's work will probably never be known. Perhaps the painting's small size simply made it attractive to an opportunist. A rare example of one of the artist's small devotional panels, *Madonna and Child with Saint Sebastian* would have been hard to sell for its true value without attracting attention.

The gallery came in for criticism: like most New Zealand public art galleries of the time it had only a skeleton staff responsible for security.[26] In 1959 few art institutions had systems that made it possible to guard each and every object – unlike today when small and particularly valuable works of art are securely fastened to walls with a T-head locking device that makes it near impossible to remove them without specialist tools. Things were slow to change and more sophisticated systems took time to arrive, often through lack of resources. In 1966 Stewart Maclennan, the director of the National Art Gallery, noted that the building had a closed-circuit television system to watch only over its most valued work, John Singleton Copley's 1771 portrait *Mrs Humphrey Devereux*, acquired the year before.

BEFORE GALLERIES HAD COLLECTION MANAGERS and digitised computer databases, keeping track of an entire collection was not easy. Even so, Auckland Art Gallery was embarrassed when in 1983 one of its own works was offered back to it for purchase. It transpired that it and three other works had been stolen from the gallery between July 1954 and December 1973.

A sixty-eight-year-old man who worked at the gallery was subsequently charged with theft of all four works and receiving stolen property. The court received statements from twenty-four witnesses. One was Eric Young, who had been a curator and registrar at the gallery during the 1970s. According to Young, the gallery's catalogue had been neither accurate nor complete during the years he worked there. Several works were unaccounted for.

In December 1982 a list of thirty-two missing works was posted in national daily newspapers in an effort to locate them. The *Auckland Star* noted:

> Works believed to be by Whistler, Dürer and Turner are among the 32 most wanted missing pictures from the Auckland Art Gallery. Nobody knows when they vanished. Their disappearance was not detected until staff catalogued the collection in the mid 1970s.

It was suggested that some of the works may have been lent to other organisations and not returned.

To distance himself from the stolen goods, the accused man had used unsuspecting art dealers to handle their sales. In one case a private collector had recognised an 1874 watercolour, *New Plymouth, Taranaki*, by J.C. Hoyte when it was offered to him by a dealer. It was returned to the gallery.

Another of the missing works, Dutch artist Petrus van Schendel's circa 1865 painting *Market woman by candle-light*, turned up in February 1983 at *Fine Victorian and Continental Pictures of the 19th and 20th Centuries*, an auction at Christie's in London. Van Schendel, known as Monsieur Chandelle, was a nineteenth-century Dutch

Romantic painter who found his niche specialising in night-time scenes that included a figure or subject brightly lit by a candle or lamp. He is represented in major European galleries, including the Rijksmuseum in Amsterdam. *Market woman by candle-light* was a part of a superb collection of art that had been bequeathed to Auckland Art Gallery in 1885 by James Tannock Mackelvie, an entrepreneur who had amassed a fortune through investments in gold mining. The painting, listed by Eric Young as missing in the 1970s, resurfaced at an auction in the early 1980s. Rodney Wilson, then director of Auckland Art Gallery, noticed it because of his strong interest in Dutch painting, but did not know it had been stolen from his own gallery.

The thief must have known what he or she was doing. The painting's relatively small size, 279 x 355 mm, would have made it easy to remove and its value meant it would fetch a good price, although the person had run a risk selling it in Auckland. Subsequently the painting ended up in Melbourne before making its way to London for the auction at Christie's. Once recognised it was withdrawn from sale and returned to Auckland Art Gallery. In 2012, *Market by candlelight*, a van Schendel painting of similar size and subject matter, sold for £57,650 at Bonhams auction house in London.

THE FORMER GALLERY EMPLOYEE was charged with the theft of *Hami Hone Ropiha (John Hobbs)*, an 1862 work by a colonial artist named William Ewart. This painting had an interesting backstory. John Hobbs had been an orderly for Governor George Grey during battles against Ngāpuhi in the north in 1845 and 1846, and a grateful Grey had controversially rewarded him with a piece of waterfront land in Auckland. The portrait of Hobbs, commissioned by Grey, had hung in Grey's home on Kawau Island until he donated it to the city in 1887 and it became the first New Zealand painting to hang in the Auckland Art Gallery.

Late in 1982 Auckland art dealer Peter Webb brought *Hami Hone Ropiha (John Hobbs)* to the gallery, thinking it might be interested in acquiring it. The fact the gallery had lost it had gone unnoticed for years.

Another of the stolen works, *Ahia, Chief of Cloudy Bay*, had been removed from the gallery before being accessioned or recorded in any way. In 1981 it was put on the market by a Dunedin dealer, Marshall Seifert, on behalf of a client, and bought by the Alexander Turnbull Library for $1,000. After the return of the John Hobbs painting to Auckland Art Gallery, Marian Minson, the curator of art at the Turnbull, began to question the provenance of *Ahia, Chief of Cloudy Bay* and whether it had been the client's to sell. She contacted Auckland Art Gallery and described the work in detail, enclosing a black and white photocopy.

The gallery assured Minson it did not own the work but Minson would discover documentation that suggested the opposite. A Mr R.A. Hodgson of Southhampton, England, was listed as the donor. In 1983 gallery director Rodney Wilson wrote to Hodgson, who confirmed in writing that he had gifted the work in 1958 via New Zealand House in London, having purchased it from a local junk shop. He had thought it should be in a New Zealand public collection.

The total value of the works allegedly stolen by the gallery's former employee was estimated at $21,500, or around $40,000 in today's money. The crime proved hard to prove: the man was found not guilty and granted permanent name suppression.

AT 5.55 ON THE MORNING OF SATURDAY, March 31, 1990 the front doors of the Auckland Art Gallery were smashed by someone using a heavy wooden cable drum. The alarms sounded but the thief or thieves had enough time to make off with four significant works: *Unloading* by Charles Tole, a 1944 painting in the Cubist style, reworked in 1976; *Landscape with Eucalyptus Tree* (undated) and *Motutapu* (circa 1908), both by Swedish-born Clas Edvard Friström; and *Shelly Beach* (1916) by Walter Wright.

The works were part of a large exhibition of 250 works, *Two Centuries of New Zealand Landscape Art*, and the thieves seemed to know what they were after: the four works were all of high value, both financially and artistically.

About three hours after the break-in, Michael Trevor Armstrong, a twenty-eight-year-old builder, approached a construction worker in nearby Lorne Street and asked for a Stanley knife. Soon afterwards he was seen a short distance away in Kitchener Street, carrying a number of paintings under his denim jacket.

Later he took a taxi to the flat of his estranged partner in the suburb of Parnell. Asked to leave, he assaulted the woman, her female friend, and a store owner. When police officers arrived to arrest him, Armstrong took them to the paintings and admitted receiving them and discarding the picture frames. At his trial he would claim he had found the paintings in Lorne Street. His defence failed and he was sentenced to ten months' imprisonment for assault and receiving stolen property. It was never entirely clear whether he had committed the robbery himself.

Three of the paintings were undamaged but *Shelly Beach* had suffered a severe three-way tear. Although the painting was later repaired, traces of the damage are still visible. The robbery was a wake-up call for the gallery staff, who had believed the front door was impenetrable.

THE THEFT AND DESECRATION of *Still on Top* holds the record as New Zealand's worst art crime. It was a senseless act carried out by a notorious criminal who gave no thought to the consequences of his actions. Sarah Hillary and her team's conservation work was remarkable, and the painting has graced the walls of the gallery regularly for more than a decade since its trauma. It remains among the most valuable paintings held in a New Zealand public collection. Worldwide, over sixty Tissot oil paintings have been sold at auction since 2000. The highest price, paid by composer Andrew Lloyd Webber, was £3,035,093 (around NZ$6.45 million) for *The Garden Bench*, a work also painted in Tissot's garden at Grove End, circa 1882.

In 2006 *Preparing for the Gala,* the companion painting to *Still on Top*, came up for auction at Christie's in London and sold for £1.69 million (around NZ$3.6 million). It had sold at Sotheby's in New York ten years earlier for US$1.65 million (NZ$2.32 million).

Works in a public art gallery are regularly revalued, both for insurance purposes and asset registers. The value of a collection is based more on artistic and intrinsic value than on possible resale price, since it is rare for works to be sold. Auckland Art Gallery's insurers, after months of negotiation, paid out around $140,000 for the conservation work on *Still on Top*, plus an additional settlement of $500,000 to 'benefit' the gallery. The gallery owned another Tissot work, an 1881 drypoint etching called *Soirée d'Été* (Summer Evening), which it had purchased in 1972. Following the settlement it purchased another of the artist's drypoint etchings,

Octobre (October), dating from 1878. Both works help place *Still on Top* in its historical and artistic context.

IN 2006, WHILE SERVING HIS SENTENCE at Rangipo Prison in the central North Island, Ricardo Sannd disappeared during his first day of work at the prison's farm. It took the police four weeks to track him down, but not before he'd stolen a BMW motorbike and a car and burgled a house. Sannd had a penchant for motorbikes; in 1996 he had taken one on a test ride from a dealer in Hamilton and never returned it. In March 2013 he was released on parole after serving fourteen years of his seventeen-year sentence. Two months later he was back inside, having helped himself to another motorbike, this time a Ducati valued at $130,000. His parole was revoked.

To date, Sannd has spent over thirty years of his adult life in prison. In 2015 he tried to claim $1.75 million in damages for unlawful detention, insisting he had spent 1,490 days too long behind bars. The claim was struck out by the court.

Because of immigration regulations, Sannd's wife Elena was never able to join him in New Zealand. She remained living in Bundaberg, a city in the Australian state of Queensland, and died there while Sannd was in jail, having never enjoyed the life of luxury he had planned for her.

ELEVEN

The copycats

EARLY IN 1988, A NEW ZEALAND COMPANY called Balfour Roofing ran an imaginative television advertisement. In a setting resembling an art gallery, an actor posed as a sculptor, complete with overalls and a beret. Around him were his creations, African animals made from corrugated iron. This was not altogether surprising as corrugated iron is a favourite roofing material in New Zealand and the advertisement could just be seen as a colourful way of advertising a product installed by Balfour. The problem was that the corrugated iron animals bore an uncanny resemblance to those produced by sculptor Jeff Thomson.

Jeff Thomson is a graduate of the University of Auckland's School of Fine Arts and started his artistic career as a painter and printmaker. In 1980, while living at a place called Portobello on Otago Peninsula, he became fascinated by roadside objects – mailboxes in particular. From making and decorating mailboxes, he moved on to sculpting animals using corrugated iron, a material readily to hand, and painting them in vivid colours. From his first sculpture, a red cow, he progressed to other animals, including elephants, giraffes and other African species. Thomson's work is highly original and distinctive.

The Balfour advertisement was too similar to be a coincidence and Thomson sought legal advice. His lawyer, Paul Davison, approached Balfour Roofing, suggesting there had been a breach of copyright under a practice known as 'passing off'. Thomson was asked by Balfour to provide detailed evidence about his practice, including how long he had been making corrugated iron animals, how many he had sold, and in which publications they had featured. The company was not satisfied and the parties went to court.

By this stage Thomson was having to spend a lot of time dealing with the matter. As Davison told the court:

> Our client has suffered and is continuing to suffer considerable embarrassment and loss of reputation. He is consistently having to explain to persons who contact him that he is not and has not been associated with either the production of the animal sculptures in the advertisement or the production of the advertisement itself.

Thomson won the case and was compensated accordingly. Today he is one of New Zealand's best-loved sculptors, and creator of some of its most iconic works, including Taihape's *Gumboot* and the elephant entrance at Auckland Zoo. From 2013 to 2016, *Corrugations: The art of Jeff Thomson*, an exhibition celebrating his work to date, toured the country, and he is represented in major collections both in New Zealand and internationally. A saloon car he clad in corrugated iron and drove for three years features in the collection of Te Papa.

IT IS ONE THING TO COPY an artist's work, but who would be brazen enough to impersonate the artist himself? Unbelievably, this has happened. Around 2004 Dean Buchanan, a west Auckland artist, made a loose arrangement with a man called Ian Malcolm Baikie. Baikie was to sell Buchanan's paintings on commission. At first everything went well: a few paintings were sold and Buchanan was paid. However, in 2006 he received unsettling reports: Baikie was said to be posing as him and even signing his paintings. He was also using Buchanan's identity to get favours such as free accommodation.

A distressed Buchanan asked for the return of all of his paintings that were still in Baikie's possession, and payment for those that Baikie had sold and not paid him for. After Baikie refused, Buchanan made a complaint to police and the case went to trial. Witnesses reported seeing Baikie pretending to be Buchanan in places as far afield as Wanaka and Karamea in the South Island and Napier in Hawke's Bay and Brown's Bay and Piha in Auckland. Baikie was described by the judge as a conman and found guilty.

It did not end there. On one occasion a downtown Auckland bar phoned Dean Buchanan. A man, later identified as Baikie, was trying to clear a $5,000 cheque in Buchanan's name. Buchanan does not drink.

Buchanan never received back any of his lost artworks; their estimated value was at least $40,000 and would be much more today.

TWELVE

Holden Heist

FOR OVER A QUARTER OF A CENTURY Elizabeth Wearn has dreamt of one day being reunited with five paintings that are dear to her. In 1992 Wearn was living in her family home, situated down a long driveway in the Auckland suburb of Remuera, when the paintings disappeared. The art collection had been acquired by her father and grandfather, and included a 1950 oil, *Still Life with Irises*, by Rata Lovell-Smith, which her father had given her shortly after her marriage in 1962. Also gone were another painting by Lovell-Smith, *Snowstorm*, painted in 1945; *Scottish Landscape with Sheep* by William Menzies Gibb (circa 1910); *Australian Landscape* by Robert H. Johnson (circa 1948); and *Fishing Boats Timaru* by Archibald Frank Nicoll, from 1932. Bedding, clothing, a television set, household appliances and several antiques were also missing.

When the police were notified they suggested that other valuable works in the home be removed temporarily for safekeeping in case the perpetrators returned to finish the job. This was good advice. A few days after the burglary, Wearn left her property on an errand.

As she turned out of her driveway and drove down the street she noticed an unfamiliar Holden car parked on the roadside. When the two occupants saw her looking at them, they drove off. Wearn followed but lost sight of the car. A neighbour later confirmed having seen the same Holden at the Wearns' house on the day of the burglary.

Elizabeth Wearn has described the crime as a dreadful and sickening episode in her life. Nothing can compensate for the loss of works of art with such strong sentimental value. Although the police followed several leads, including investigating recent visitors to the house, the case remains unsolved and the paintings have never surfaced.

It is possible they have come up for sale but New Zealand does not have a registry of missing art works, something that would have helped alert prospective buyers and auction houses. The only evidence that the paintings ever existed are photographs held by Wearn, but they are of poor quality. The police file of this case no longer even exists, presumably discarded after seven years had passed.

Cases like this are the tip of a very large iceberg. There are undoubtedly many more stories yet to be told: I hope the ones in this book will inspire others to be unearthed and exposed.

Art crime is not easy to research. In my experience, victims are rarely keen to share their stories. Others who may have information will often try to withhold it, and even actively avoid the person doing the research. As Peter Ireland, who discovered that the Lindauer portrait at Waikato Museum was a fake, noted: 'There's a conspiracy of silence in the art world over these things.'

I was never able, for example, to discover whether the reward for information about the stolen Tissot, *Still on Top*, was ever paid.

There will be people who know about the whereabouts of the numerous missing works by Edward Bullmore and the paintings stolen from Elizabeth Wearn, but they too are not talking.

Crime will continue to mar the art world. With the advent of ever more sophisticated copying processes, fraud will increase: the ability to copy a work and pass it off as original is getting easier and the rewards are alluring. In 2016 Dick Frizzell, a renowned New Zealand artist, was annoyed to find laser prints of his work being sold on the Trade Me auction site. By removing the prints from the frames, the culprit, a Wellington picture framer, was identified; legal action was avoided when the framer agreed to meet terms laid out by Frizzell and his business partner.

But while technology is making it easier to forge works it is also, ironically, increasing the chances of the forgeries being detected: the internet acts as a clearing house for information about missing and fraudulent artworks and perpetrators of art crimes. Some countries now have police squads dedicated to finding and prosecuting the criminals. Private organisations also act as detectives, locating missing works – particularly those stolen by the Nazis in the Second World War – and mediating their return to the original owners or their descendants.

Educating not only legitimate dealers and auction houses but also art buyers, including private collectors, on how to avoid rip-offs is vital. Anyone considering buying a work of art needs to be vigilant about provenance and authenticity. Most people will have a motor vehicle checked over by a mechanic before finalising a purchase, or a building inspection carried out when buying real estate, but art is different. Swept away by the beauty of a work or excited by the frenzy of an auction, a buyer will all too often throw caution to the wind. Taking more time is essential. Careful investigation is the best protection against fraud.

ART THEFT AND FRAUD MAY SEEM MINOR and peripheral crimes, but are they? As individuals, we value art. Domestic collections take time and hard-earned money to develop. Irreplaceable family heirlooms are invested with emotional value. And as a nation, art helps define who we are. National artworks and collections are a country's face to the rest of the world. When important works are removed or destroyed, this chips away at a country's history and cultural life.

Art crime in New Zealand does not in general receive special treatment from the police, and many would argue this is appropriate when it is set against crimes such as rape and murder. When art criminals are caught and convicted, sentencing varies. Under New Zealand's 2003 Crimes Amendment Act, the sentence is to be based on the monetary value of the artwork in question: emotional and sentimental values do not count. Ricardo Sannd was given nearly seventeen years in prison for a raft of crimes, including armed robbery of the valuable Tissot painting from Auckland Art Gallery. By comparison, for impersonating Dean Buchanan and selling works without paying him, Ian Malcolm Baikie received only 150 hours' community service and was instructed to pay the artist $5,000. When Baikie's lawyer argued that his client was a sickness beneficiary and therefore strapped for cash, reparation payments were set at at a mere $20 a week spread out over five years. Although this was a light sentence given the years of grief Baikie had given Buchanan, at the time of writing Baikie had lodged an appeal.

The two men who absconded with Bing Dawe's *Tuna* from Auckland Botanic Gardens also received community service – 60 hours and 100 hours respectively – and were ordered to pay reparation of $1,500 each. They failed to turn up to court for the hearing and were given a further 40 hours' community service.

The uniqueness of art crimes makes it difficult to standardise sentences. Slovenian criminologists Bojan Dobovšek and Boštjan Slak have argued that the public is likely to want harsher punishment for a criminal who has targeted an artwork in a public collection than for someone who has stolen a work from a wealthy collector. The latter act is seen as relatively harmless, even though the object may be irreparable or irreplaceable.

Sentencing also varies considerably among countries. Thomas McShane, a former FBI undercover art sleuth, presented a fascinating scenario in his 2006 book *Stolen Masterpiece Tracker*. If *Mona Lisa* were to be stolen from The Louvre, sold in New York for US$350 million, and the perpetrator caught the following week, he or she would be given something like an eighteen-month sentence for the 'sale and transportation of stolen property'. However, if *Mona Lisa* were the property of an American museum and stolen, under a 1994 statute covering theft of major artwork the thief would face a ten-year prison sentence, applicable to thefts of artworks over one hundred years old and/or valued at US$100,000 or more.

Historically, art forgers have received light punishments. The notorious German fraudster Wolfgang Beltracchi and his wife Helene Beltracchi made and sold hundreds of forged works, claiming they were newly discovered works by famous artists, including Picasso, which Helene had inherited. In 2011 they received prison sentences of six and four years respectively for forging and selling fourteen artworks for US$45 million. They served their sentences in an open prison: the couple had day jobs and returned to the prison at night. During and after their incarceration they published two books, participated in a documentary film about themselves, *Beltracchi – The Art of Forgery*, and continued to paint. Following his release in 2015 Wolfgang Beltracchi held an exhibition of paintings with his own signature and price tags in the high thousands. German art experts have tracked down a further sixty suspected Beltracchi fakes, and Beltracchi himself has reported seeing his works hanging in major galleries. He has remained unapologetic.

Then there are the criminals who get away scot-free. Elmyr de Hory, a mysterious Hungarian forger who is believed to have sold more than a thousand fake artworks to major art galleries, was never convicted of forgery because it could not be proved he had made any of his forged works on Spanish soil. (He lived on the island of Ibiza, one of the Balearic Islands, an autonomous community of Spain.) In 1976, after years of legal wrangling, France finally secured de Hory's extradition to stand trial there. Fearing he would be killed in prison, de Hory committed suicide by overdosing on sleeping pills. Since then researchers have been trying to figure out his real identity. Meanwhile, many of his fakes hang undetected in galleries around the world.

De Hory's reach extended to New Zealand. In October 2014 two works signed by him were put up for sale at Cordy's Fine Art and Antique Auctioneers in Auckland. While in the style of Claude Monet, they were clearly marketed as having been painted by de Hory. I sent an art crime colleague a link to a local newspaper article about the works and he forwarded it to an American curator with specialist knowledge of de Hory.

Within hours I received an email: the works were forgeries made by a London bookmaker, Ken Talbot. The source of this information was a man called Mark Forgy, who had been de Hory's apprentice on Ibiza and had an intimate knowledge of the forger's work, which he had relayed in a self-published book *The Forger's Apprentice: Life with the World's Most Notorious Artist*. That de Hory's works were considered worth forging demonstrates an irony: a famous forger's works can themselves become valuable artworks.

This was not the end of the story. Just a few weeks later the works were again offered for auction at Cordy's. This time they were labelled: 'Artist unknown after Elmyr de Hory (Hungary 1906–1976) after Claude Monet.' They sold for $1,000 and $1,800 respectively.

In New Zealand, the two men who illegally sold works by Edward Bullmore without remitting the proceeds to the artist's widow, and who 'lost' more than 150 works that have never been recovered, also escaped without charge or conviction. Such a failure of justice can be the result of a lack of police resources to carry out a proper investigation, a lack of priority given to alleged offences, or a lack of the necessary specialist knowledge within the police to detect art crimes and prosecute the offenders. Additionally, if too much time passes, a case will usually fall in priority and become even less likely to be resolved.

WHEN ART CRIMINALS ARE PROFILED, patterns emerge. Dutch psychologist Gerrit Breeuwsma, who has studied the relationship between art and psychology, has reported that offenders are commonly male, single or recently divorced, and may have a history of mental problems. They may also have experienced some kind of traumatic event, have a penchant for fraud, or be artists who have failed to gain recognition for their own work and have discovered a skill for copying the work of others.

But there are always exceptions to the stereotype. In March 2013 a woman in her mid seventies walked into the Lakes District Museum and Art Gallery in the small South Island town of Arrowtown. She checked the hanging devices on several works and then deftly lifted a quilt by a local artist, Alison Naylor, off the wall, stuffed it in her bag and departed. What she didn't know was that her movements were being filmed on a closed-circuit television camera linked directly to the local police station. The CCTV photograph was rapidly circulated on social media and the next day the woman was arrested in the town of Te Anau, 180 kilometres away.

She was a British tourist on a bus tour. Other passengers had noted her propensity for being light-fingered; she was said to have been seen stealing several other items, including an object made of pounamu, valuable New Zealand greenstone. The quilt was never returned. When questioned, the woman said she had felt guilty and disposed of it. It was possible that before being caught she had mailed it back to Britain. She was made to pay $695 for the quilt but did not apologise. Next day she left the country.

The ease with which the theft had been carried out raises the question of how art should be displayed. Cordoning off a work or putting it behind glass can diminish the viewer's experience. A fibre artwork such as Naylor's quilt needs to be seen up close to appreciate the materials and detail, as do most works of art. And there's another problem: giving certain works special protection can signal that they are the most valuable ones in an exhibition and so increase their appeal to criminals.

MANY TIMES DURING THE COURSE of researching and writing this book I have returned to the concept of value, which is central to the way art is perceived. Essentially, it is the value associated with a work that triggers the crime. But perceived value is subjective and, as Noah Charney has noted, 'amorphous and sharklike: it moves constantly with the times, even from one day to the next'.

And value can be influenced by outside factors. A tiny 1654 Dutch painting, *The Goldfinch*, by Carel Fabritius had quietly hung in the Mauritshuis, an art museum in The Hague, for well over a century. In 2013 a popular American novelist, Donna Tartt, published a book of the same name with a plot based around the painting. When the book became a best-seller and won the Pulitzer Prize, *The Goldfinch* rocketed in value and in reputation. In 2014 the painting was lent for a three-month exhibition at The Frick Collection in New York, where it was viewed by 230,000 visitors. The value of *The Goldfinch* is now estimated to be US$3 million.

Epilogue

ART CRIME IS A BURGEONING FIELD of study. Researchers from many countries come together each year at a conference in Italy of the Association of Research for Crimes against Art, where numerous cases are presented by detectives, art historians, writers, lawyers and independent scholars.

In 2015 the New Zealand Art Crime Research Trust was launched in an effort to increase awareness of art crime in this country, where many crimes remain unsolved or unreported, or have been hushed up so as not to encourage copycatting. It is possible that people who have missing artworks or know of other crimes involving art will now be encouraged to come forward and report them. An area where there is much yet to be documented is crimes against taonga Māori. There is a great need to have these precious items returned to their rightful owners, and to protect taonga against unlawful or culturally insensitive replication.

I hope potential purchasers of art will be spurred to undertake in-depth research before they buy a particular work, especially one at the high end of value. If a work lacks provenance, or the provenance is skimpy, be suspicious. Take the time to consult an expert.

I also urge owners of artworks to fully protect them. Make sure they are well documented with photographs, front and back, and keep a copy of the images on a secure site online and in a physical place other than your home. In the case of fire or theft, if you do not have evidence it can be your word against the insurers.

Insure your works wisely by having a valuation carried out by a reputable and registered valuer. Major auction houses will do this for a modest fee. No matter how small or large your collection, making your own catalogue is also useful. As well as a high-quality photographic image, include such information as the title of the work, size, medium, artist details, provenance, any distinguishing features (including damage and repair), and the signature. Preventive measures are less time-consuming, and less upsetting than trying to replace or repair art when something untoward has happened to it.

And a word of warning: if you gift a work to a public collection of any kind make sure you ask for and receive a receipt. Artist Michael Smither told me that over the years he had gifted many original screenprints to New Plymouth's Govett-Brewster Gallery, only to find recently that many of the works are no longer in the gallery's collection. He had not insisted on receipts or letters of gifting.

Be a little wary of the internet. Real estate is now marketed extensively online. Anyone actively looking for an artwork or stealing to order can use photos of properties on real estate websites to peruse domestic collections. At the same time, real estate websites can help to locate missing art. This occurred in March 2014 when someone in Auckland searching on the internet for a property in another part of the country spotted a missing sculpture. The 1995 stainless steel work, *Phoenix Rising*, by artist Keith Simpson had been stolen in June 2004 from outside a community library in the Auckland suburb of Epsom. The thieves had gone to some effort to remove the two-metre-tall sculpture, which was valued at $15,000. When all hope of finding it had been lost, it had been replaced with a second, slightly larger version by the same artist.

Police uplifted the stolen sculpture from the upstairs loft of a sleepout in the house, which was for sale in the small village of Rangataua, adjacent to Tongariro National Park. Charging anyone with the theft proved difficult. The owners of the property were now based in Australia. They said that when they had taken possession in 2005 the previous owners had left behind several items, including skis, furniture and the sculpture. The house had previously been used for short-term holiday rentals and numerous people had stayed there. The motive for the robbery remains a mystery.

In March 2015 *Phoenix Rising* was returned to the Albert-Eden Local Board in Auckland, whose territory included Epsom. The board decided to gift it to Great Barrier Island, where Simpson had been instrumental in setting up a community-based gallery, and it was unveiled there in May that year.

Meanwhile, in the beautiful Christchurch Art Gallery – which replaced the McDougall in 2003 and has been itself restored after sustaining damage in Christchurch's devastating 2010 and 2011 earthquakes – *Psyche*'s empty frame remains in the storeroom, a poignant reminder of an artwork that, like so many, has disappeared without trace.

ACKNOWLEDGEMENTS

During the course of my research many people have assisted me. I am indebted to the following art professionals, academics, collectors, archivists, police officers and lawyers who were generous with their time and information and willingly shared their stories: Roger Blackley, Justin Boroughs, Ron Brownson, Dean Buchanan, Marianna Bullmore, Dr Noah Charney, John Collie, Professor Raewyn Dalziel, Paul Davison, QC, Bing Dawe, Senior Constable Lane Demchy, Carla Durbè, Garth Gallaway, Dr Catherine Gardner, Dr Bev Gatenby, Dame Jenny Gibbs, William Gibson, Jonathan Gooderham, Arthur and Mary Hackett, Catherine Hammond, former detective Rex Hawkins, Sarah Hillary, Graeme and Susan Horsley, Peter Ireland, Tim Jones, Dr Peter Lineham, Caroline McBride, William McCahon, Olivia McLeavey, Detective Sergeant Dorothy McPhail, Cherie Meecham, Penney Moir, Trevor Morley, Luisa Morozzi, Jenny Neligan, Ben Plumbly, Dr Rebecca Rice, Neil Roberts, Michael Smither, Terry Stringer, Jeff Thomson, John Timmins, Judge Arthur Tompkins, Associate Professor Linda Tyler, Elizabeth Wearn and Philip Woollaston. I am grateful to Philippa Howcroft, who read my manuscript at a very early stage and encouraged me to continue writing. This book would not have been possible without the wonderful team at Awa Press. I am extremely grateful to publisher and editor Mary Varnham and production manager Emma Wolff.

Last but not least, thanks to my husband David and our children Harry and Lucy for their engagement with this project. Lucy deserves particular mention for helping me research archival material.

ENDNOTES

1 *Art Crime*, John E. Conklin: Praeger, Westport, Connecticut, 1994.

2 In November 2014 the Kunstmuseum Bern in Switzerland accepted several hundred works from the Gurlitt collection in accordance with the provisions of Gurlitt's will. Other works were to remain in Germany until their rightful ownership could be established.

3 New York art collectors and philanthropists Julian and Josie Robertson gifted fifteen works to the Auckland Art Gallery. They included works by Paul Cézanne, Pablo Picasso, Henri Matisse, Paul Gauguin and Piet Mondrian. The gift is to date is the largest ever made to an art museum in Australasia.

4 A stretcher is a wooden frame that sits within the outer frame of a painting and is used to create tension to make the canvas taut.

5 Both in private collections.

6 When John Timmins went to retrieve the works over two years later, he had a duplicate Carnet made to pre-empt further difficulties around their export from Italy.

7 This sculpture was the subject of New Zealand artist Edward Bullmore's 1959 painting *Perseus*.

8 According to an article in *New Zealand Listener*, Johanan Vitta believed the works to be valued at US$800, 000. The value used here is the 1999 auction estimate.

9 'The odyssey of two Florentine Impressionist paintings': www.firenzemadeintuscany.com.

10 Farsetti Gallery, Italy, November 1, 2014, Lot 838.

11 www.corrierepl.it/2015/07/11/silvestro-lega-il-maestro-della-luce

12 Tim Wilson would later co-author the autobiography of art fraudster Karl Sim.

13 Solpah and Butex are brand names.

14 It wasn't until 1949 that temporary exhibitions were mounted and the permanent collection began to rotate to accommodate them.

15 In the 1950s this window and others had metal security bars fixed to them. As this coincided with the gallery taking touring exhibitions it may have felt the need to upgrade security.

16 In 1981 Rotorua Art Gallery hosted a posthumous exhibition, *Edward Bullmore: Drawing from Life*. Posters of the exhibition contained a pencil drawing of a foreshortened, seated female nude with a tailor's dummy. Many businesses refused to display the poster and members of the public complained about the 'indecent image'. Rotorua public relations officer Bob Lowe was quoted as saying, 'Our job … is to create a favourable image or impression of Rotorua. The poster was distasteful to some people. They can go to the gallery for art or that type of thing.'

17 Confusingly this work has also been referred to incorrectly as *Portrait of Jacky*. The portrait also goes by the titles *Creation* and *Creation (Reassurance)*.

18 Mr V is not his real name.

19 It was reported on stuff.co.nz in 2007 that Mr V was a leading member of a gang that stole whiteware to order from houses under construction. Over three trials, convictions were secured for over $300,000 worth of stolen goods. Mr V was found guilty of thirty-four charges and ordered to serve at least three years in prison. His wife was sentenced to 250 hours' community service.

20 The missing works were valued by Neil Roberts, the former senior curator at Robert McDougall Art Gallery, who was then the owner/operator of Independent Art Valuations. The value of works whose location was known were used as a guide. As Edward Bullmore had worked in series it was easy enough to get a feel for valuing the missing works, and the family had images of some as Bullmore had routinely taken photos and colour slides of his works. A missing work on paper of a female figure of a certain size would, for example, have a similar value to one that Roberts sighted. Edward Bullmore also had standard sizes for works on paper, making the valuations of these easier.

21 Because of the restraints of exhibition spaces, *Portrait of Jacqui* was not exhibited at Te Papa until 2013.

22 Te Pātaka Whakaahua – The Lindauer Gallery at Whanganui Regional Museum is a dedicated gallery space for a collection of Lindauer portraits.

23 Born Anthony Ricardo Urry in 1950, Ricardo Sannd has gone by various other names, including Anthony Ricardo Sannds, Ricardo Genovese, Ricardo Romanov, Anthony Arden and Anthony Sannd. Genovese is the name of a well-known Mafia family. Elena Romanov, born in 1954, was also known by several other names, including Elena Vladimirovna Bath.

24 *Weekend Review* of *The New Zealand Herald* reported in August 1999: 'Doodlings found by the police at the isolated house … suggested that Sannd needed $3.7 million to provide the grand lifestyle he wanted for them both.'

25 I could not get a definitive answer from gallery staff, both former and current, as to whether this reward was ever paid. Several newspaper reports at the time suggested it was going to be. Auckland Art Gallery was unable to confirm this.

26 Security staff are still often paid the least on an art gallery team, even though they are responsible for the institution's core assets, the collection.

SOURCES

Introduction

'Recovery rate for stolen art as low as 1.5%': Melanie Gerlis and Javier Pes, *The Art Newspaper* 252, December 2013.

Kathryn Ryan, interview with the author: *Nine to Noon* , Radio New Zealand, August 5, 2013.

One: Gold from Goldies

'Goldie portrait mystery grows': *The Dominion Post*, October 25, 2008.

Art Crime, John E. Conklin: Praeger, Westport, Connecticut, 1994.

Goldie, Roger Blackley: Auckland Art Gallery, Auckland, 1997.

Policing Two Peoples: A History of Police in the Bay of Plenty 1867–1992, Jinty Rorke: New Zealand Police, Wellington, 1993.

'Curator's report on return of Goldie paintings stolen from Gallery in September 1973', George Packwood: Archives of Museum of New Zealand Te Papa Tongarewa.

Author's email correspondence with Christina Wilkinson, Auckland Grammar School, September 4, 2009.

'Stolen Goldie slipped back at secret rendezvous': *The Evening Post*, December 22, 1981.

'Recovery rate for stolen art as low as 1.5%': *The Art Newspaper* 252, December 2013.

'Precarious world of precious art', Nigel Benson: *The Otago Daily Times*, February 8, 2008.

Author's conversation with Jonathan Gooderham, September 15, 2011.

'Art thieves snatch Goldie, McCahons in library raid', Elizabeth Binning and Anne Gibson: *The New Zealand Herald*, January 6, 2007.

'Stolen artefacts return home': stuff.co.nz, October 27, 2007.

Author's email correspondence with Andrew Clifford, University of Auckland, September 4, 2009.

'Goldie, Charles Frederick', Roger Blackley, in *Dictionary of New Zealand Biography*, volume 3, Claudia Orange, general editor: Auckland University Press, 1996; also at http://www.teara.govt.nz/en/biographies/3g14/goldie-charles-frederick

Two: The forger

Art Crime, John E. Conklin: Praeger, Westport, Connecticut, 1994.

Good as Goldie: The amazing story of New Zealand's most famous art forger, Karl Sim (Carl Goldie) and Tim Wilson: Hachette, Auckland, 2002.

'Alas, now Gone as Goldie', Mr Sterile Assembly: https://mrsterileassembly.wordpress.com/tag/karl-sim/, October 24, 2013.

'Sim signed masterpiece – expert': *The Evening Post,* July 1986.

A Closer Look: Deceptions & Discoveries, Marjorie E Wieseman: National Gallery, London, 2010.

False Impressions: The Hunt for Big-Time Art Fakes, Thomas Hoving: Simon & Schuster, New York, 1997.

'Final sign-off for Goldie imitator', Andrew Koubaridis: *The New Zealand Herald*, October 25, 2013.

'Creative, crooked or cute?: *Times Live*, http://www.times.co.nz/our-homes-today/creative-crooked-or-cute.html?limitstart=2, September 29, 2008.

'Welcome Morsels draws on popular sentimentality', Penelope Jackson: *The Press*, July 23, 1991.

The Asian, Heather Straka: Dunedin Public Art Gallery touring exhibition, 2010.

'Fake Art', Lloyd Jones: *Wellington City Magazine*, September 1985.

Goldie, Roger Blackley: Auckland Art Gallery and David Bateman, Auckland, 1997.

The Big Picture, Hamish Keith: Godwit, Auckland, 2007.

Author's correspondence with William Gibson, September 2013.

Three: The Macchiaioli affair

New Zealand Medical Services in the Middle East and Italy, Colonel T. Duncan M. Stout: War History Branch, Department of Internal Affairs, Wellington, 1956.

'Find thrills gallery', Lee Harris: *Otago Daily Times*: December 22, 1994.

'The Macchiaioli Affair: Lost and Found in Italy', John Timmins, in *Art Antiquity and Law*: volume 7, issue 2, June 2002.

Author's email correspondence with Peter Entwisle, June 2013.

'Art crime not always black and white', Peter Entwisle: *Otago Daily Times*, November 15, 2008.

'Five Macchiaioli in the business of war': *The Art Newspaper*, February 21, 1998.

'Be bold, buy old and international', Peter Entwisle: *Otago Daily Times*, January 11, 2010.

Stolen: The Gallery of Missing Masterpieces, Jonathan Webb: Madison Press, Toronto, 2008.

'Gallery's paintings seized in war booty row', Naomi Larkin: *The New Zealand Herald*, April 4, 1998.

Author's conversation with John Timmins, July 1, 2013.

'Looted: The Dunedin Public Art Gallery finds itself accused of receiving art stolen by the Nazis', Desmond O'Grady: *New Zealand Listener*, May 15, 1999.

'Privacy Policy', *Vitoronzo Pastore*: http://www.pastorevito.it/privacy-policy/.

Author's email correspondence with Luisa Morozzi, December 30, 2014.

Four: Caveat emptor

'Artist spurns former friend and fakes': *The New Zealand Herald*, October 26, 1996.

Author's conversation with Philip Woollaston, July 2014.

Author's conversation with Olivia McLeavey, August 2014.

Interview with Jane Evans and Kerry Aberhart: *Morning Report*, Radio New Zealand, November 26, 1996.

'Crook Art', Tim Wilson: *New Zealand Listener*, January 25, 1997.

Author's correspondence from Philip Woollaston, October 2014.

Beneath the Surface: McCahon's materials and techniques 1954–66, Sarah Hillary and Kendrah Morgan: Auckland Art Gallery, Auckland, 2000.

Canterbury Painting in the 1990s, Felicity Milburn: Robert McDougall Art Gallery, Christchurch, 2000.

'Auction scene', John Perry: *Art News New Zealand*, Spring 2014.

'McCahon pulled from sale', Kim Knight: stuff.co.nz, August 3, 2014.

'Auction house stand by treatment of McCahon painting', Kim Knight: stuff.co.nz, August 10, 2014.

Five: The loss of Psyche

Author's correspondence with Neil Roberts, August 5, 2013.

'Hopes dashed of recovering stolen painting': *The Press*, July 5, 1982.

'"Psyche" considered to be part of hoax', Peter Comer: *The Press*: November 5, 1982.

'The way it was: "Leda and the Swan"', Neil Roberts in *Bulletin 118*: Robert McDougall Art Gallery, 1999.

'Mythical swan photo taken down after "bestiality" fears': *The Telegraph*: April 28, 2012.

Official record of the New Zealand International Exhibition of Arts and Industries held at Christchurch, 1906–7, J. Cowan: Government Printer, Wellington, 1910.

Handbook to the Picture Gallery of Works of Art, Melbourne International Exhibition, 1880–81, Stephen Thompson: P.E. Reynolds, 1880.

Six: Urewera Mural

Author's conversation with Dame Jenny Gibbs, March 2014.

'Te Kaha accomplice jailed for theft': *The Dominion*, February 6, 1999.

'Iti uses look-alike to confuse police', Geoff Mercer: *Whakatane Beacon*, December 11, 2014.

Floor talk by Tame Iti, Whakatāne Museum, December 2013.

'Te Kaha, "to make restitution to the art world"': *The New Zealand Herald*, December 19, 1998.

Art Crime, John E. Conklin: Praeger, Westport, Connecticut, 1994.

The Irish Game: A True Story of Crime and Art, Matthew Hart: Walker and Company, New York, 2004.

Author's correspondence with William McCahon, March 2014.

'Spear attack mars McCahon Urewera Mural return', Eleanor Black: *The New Zealand Herald*: September 23, 2000.

Floor talk by Jonathan Mane-Wheoki, Whakatāne Museum, January 2014.

'Living in Time: A Day at the Footie', Ian Wedde: Museums Aotearoa 'Engaging Practices' symposium, Auckland, 1997.

***Seven*: All in the family**

'Hot Art', Tony Wall: *The Sunday Star Times*, March 18, 2012.

'Under-fire art dealer defends his actions', Tony Wall: *The Sunday Star-Times*, April 8, 2012.

'Brother in court as feud over artist's legacy flares': *The New Zealand Herald*, June 22.

'Art dealer acknowledges "missing" Bullmore was sold', Tony Wall: *The Sunday Star-Times*, March 25, 2012.

Email correspondence from Margaret Callanan to Garth Gallaway, May 25, 2009.

Correspondence from Detective Mike Bridgman to Marianna Bullmore, August 10, 2011.

Eight: Lot No. 60

Article by Ngahiraka Mason in *ART TOI: New Zealand Art at Auckland Art Gallery Toi o Tamaki*, Ron Brownson, editor: Auckland Art Gallery Toi o Tamaki, Auckland, 2011.

'Art world full of forgery "shenanigans", artist says', Anna Wallis: *The New Zealand Herald*, November 1, 2012.

Interview with Roger Blackley: *Afternoons with Jim Mora*, Radio New Zealand, October 19, 2012.

'Art adviser rubbishes fake painting claims', Chris Gardner: stuff.co.nz , January 22, 2013.

'Fake Lindauer's origins lost to history', Chris Gardner: *Waikato Times*, November 11, 2012.

Author's conversation with Sarah Hillary, Auckland Art Gallery Toi o Tamaki, October 2, 2013.

Conservation Report of Kewene Te Haho, Sarah Hillary: Auckland Art Gallery Toi o Tamaki, Auckland, September 28, 2012.

'Painting of Tainui chief judged a fake', Chris Gardner: stuff.co.nz, October 2012.

'Law Destroys Fake Art', Karen Abidi: *The Fortnightly Review*, June 17, 2010.

'Judge orders destruction of fake art', Gabriella Coslovich: *The Age*, June 2, 2010,

'Turnbull Library admits it bought a fake Lindauer': *Nine to Noon*, Radio New Zealand, October 9, 2015.

Nine: Pania of the Reef

'Pania of the Reef: The Statue', V. May Cottrell: *Te Ao Hou The New World* 10, April 1955.

'MP retreats on Pania Ransom', Jarrod Booker: *The New Zealand Herald*, October 29, 2005.

'Thieves use crane and lorry to steal £3m Henry Moore sculpture for scrap', Robin Stummer: *The Independent*, December 18, 2005.

'Stolen bronze eel sculpture recovered', Nikki Papatsoumas: *The New Zealand Herald*, July 22, 2014.

'Bronzed eel found badly damaged': *Checkpoint*, Radio New Zealand, July 22, 2014.

'Vandals paint Little Bull statue': *Waikato Times*, May 16, 1968.

'The Significance of Studying and Investigation Art Crime: Old Reasons, New World', Bojan Dobovšek and Boštjan Slak: *Varstvoslovje Journal of Criminal Justice and Security*, 2011.

Ten: For love of Elena

'Court hears of bid to ransom oil painting': *The New Zealand Herald*, June 30, 2000.

'A Tissot, A Tissot, we all fall down', Tim Wilson: *Metro*, November 1999.

'NZ's biggest art heist – culprit out of jail and talking', Kirsty Wynn and Jonathan Milne: *The New Zealand Herald*, March 18, 2012.

'"Brutal" art robber sentenced': *The New Zealand Herald*, June 30, 2000.

'Tissot robber tells all', Jonathan Milne: *The New Zealand Herald*, March 18, 2012.

'Valuable paintings subject of charges': *Otago Daily Times*, February 8, 1984.

Tissot: Still on Top http://www.aucklandartgallery.com/whats-on/exhibition/tissot-still-on-top

'Insurance settlement reached on Tissot's *Still on Top*': media release, Auckland Art Gallery Toi O Tamaki, Auckland, 1998.

'Art thief seeks compo for too much time in jail', Paul Easton: stuff.co.nz, July 15, 2015.

Eleven: Holden heist

'Art world full of forgery "shenanigans", artist says', Anna Wallis: *The New Zealand Herald*, November 1, 2012.

Stolen: the Gallery of Missing Masterpieces, Jonathan Webb: Madison Press, Toronto, 2008.

Correspondence to A.F. Grant and D. Clapshaw on behalf of Jeff Thomson from P. J. Davison, Keegan Alexander Tedcastle and Friedlander, March 8, 1988.

'Impersonator ordered to pay artist $5000', Rob Kidd, *The New Zealand Herald*, November 25, 2014,

Correspondence with Dr Catherine Gardner, New Zealand Police, September 25, 2015.

Stolen Masterpiece Tracker, Thomas McShane with Dary Matera: Barricade Books, New Jersey, 2006.

'Art forger's masterpieces in city sale', Kurt Bayer: *The New Zealand Herald*, October 4, 2014.

The Forger's Apprentice: Life with the World's Most Notorious Artist, Mark Forgy: CreateSpace Independent Publishing Platform, 2012.

'The Significance of Studying and Investigation Art Crime: Old Reasons, New World', Bojan Dobovšek and Boštjan Slak: *Varstvoslovje Journal of Criminal Justice and Security*, 2011.

'De rust van het onherstelbare; een kleine psychologie van het kunstvandalisme (Themanummer: Kunst en criminaliteit)', G. Breeuwsma: *Justitiële Verkenningen* 1 (23).

Author's conversation with David Clarke, Lakes District Museum and Gallery, Arrowtown, July 18, 2014.

The Art of Forgery, Noah Charney: Phaidon Press, 2015.

Vermeer, Rembrandt, and Hals: Masterpieces of Dutch Painting from the Mauritshuis: exhibition at Frick Collection, New York, October 22, 2013 to January 19, 2014.

Fabritius and the Goldfinch, Deborah Davis: Kindle Single, 2014.

ILLUSTRATION CREDITS

Section one

Wakey, Wakey, Wakey by John Reynolds, 2012, in exhibition at City Gallery Wellington: photograph by Kate Whitley, 2012

Derelict by Edward Bullmore, 1957: Tauranga City Council / Marianna Bullmore

C.F. Goldie in his studio with chief Patara Te Tuhi, 1901: Museum of New Zealand Te Papa Tongarewa; photograph by Robert Love

The Evening Post reporter Catherine Perry holding a poster depicting lost Goldie paintings, October 4, 1973: Alexander Turnbull Library, Wellington, New Zealand, EP/1973/4353/24A-F

Pipi Puzzled by C.F. Goldie, 1919: Museum of New Zealand Te Papa Tongarewa

Welcome Morsels by Leonard Charles Nightingale, date unknown: Christchurch Art Gallery Te Puna o Waiwhetu

Portrait of Sir George Grey by Louis John Steele, date unknown, hanging in the auditorium of Auckland Grammar School, 1980: Auckland Grammar School

Karl Sim, aka Carl Feodor Goldie, at his Hatfields Beach retreat, 4 November 2005: Fairfax NZ; photograph by David White

Two head studies of a young girl by Karl Sim, acquired by Museum of New Zealand Te Papa Tongarewa c. 1980. Originally attributed to Petrus van der Velden: Museum of New Zealand Te Papa Tongarewa

Study of a young boy by Karl Sim, acquired by Museum of New Zealand Te Papa Tongarewa c. 1980. Originally attributed to Petrus van der Velden: Museum of New Zealand Te Papa Tongarewa

Sketch of woman reading by Petrus van der Velden, c. 1872: Museum of New Zealand Te Papa Tongarewa

Sketch of man reading by Petrus van der Velden, 1873: Museum of New Zealand Te Papa Tongarewa

Mural of Ina Te Papatahi by Owen Dippie, Tauranga 2012; a copy of C.F. Goldie's 1902 portrait of the Ngāpuhi chieftainess: photograph by Daniel du Bern

Woman sitting by a window sewing by Silvestro Lega, 1872: collection of the Dunedin Public Art Gallery

The baker's shop at Settignano by Telemaco Signorini (undated)

Section two

Orange Glass by Peter Siddell, 2005: name of photographer withheld by request

Orange Glass under ultraviolet light: Auckland Art Gallery Toi o Tamaki, photograph by Ingrid Ford

Rossano Fan, c. 2011: Richard Riddiford; photographer unknown

Tasman Bay by Toss Woollaston, c. 1990, oil on canvas: Toss Woollaston Trust / Sally Hunt Fine Art

Nelson Landscape, watercolour by Rossano Fan; sketch attributed to Toss Woollaston, 1976: David Hamilton Photography

Elias by Colin McCahon, 1959, as printed in Webb's auction house catalogue 384, July 31, 2014

The Fountain by William A. Breakspeare, 1883: collection of Christchurch Art Gallery Te Puna o Waiwhetu

Leda and the Swan by Adolphe Jourdan, etching of original painting; purchased by Neil Roberts and gifted to Christchurch Art Gallery Te Puna o Waiwhetu: Christchurch Art Gallery Te Puna o Waiwhetu

Black and white photograph of *Psyche* (image reversed), a 1902 painting by Solomon J. Solomon: Christchurch Art Gallery Te Puna o Waiwhetu; photograph taken 1932

Āniwaniwa Visitor Centre in Te Urewera National Park with Colin McCahon's *Urewera Mural* returned to its original position: photograph by Craig Martin, 2004

Tame Iti in front of *Urewera Mural* at Te Kōputu a Te Whanga a Toi – Whakatāne Library and Exhibition Centre. On the right is Kay Boreham, museum and art exhibition coordinator: *Whakatane Beacon*, December 8, 2013; photograph by Geoff Mercer

Transition No. 6 by Edward Bullmore, 1961: Tauranga Art Gallery Toi Tauranga / Marianna Bullmore

The Gates by Edward Bullmore, 1959: Christchurch Art Gallery Te Puna o Waiwhetu

Jacqueline Bullmore holding a self-portrait of her husband Edward Bullmore, titled *The Seer*, March 7, 2012: Fairfax New Zealand

Art dealer Pat Condon, March 7, 2012: Fairfax New Zealand

Portrait of Jacqui by Edward Bullmore, 1959: Museum of New Zealand Te Papa Tongarewa / Marianna Bullmore

Section three

Gottfried Lindauer, c. 1899: Alexander Turnbull Library, Wellington, New Zealand, the Partridge Collection of Māori paintings, PUBL-0092-001

Portrait of Haoni or Hamiora Maioha, artist unknown. Originally attributed to Gottfried Lindauer and purchased by the Alexander Turnbull Library, April 2013

Kewene Te Haho, Gottfried Lindauer: Auckland Art Gallery Toi o Tāmaki, gift of Mr H.E. Partridge, 1915

Reclining Nude, artist and date unknown; originally attributed to Marc Chagall

Big Blue Lavender Bay, Mohamed Aman Siddique, c. 2007; originally attributed to Brett Whiteley

Statue of boy and Opo the dolphin on Opononi beachfront: Richard Joseph, 2010

Terry Stringer 2008 sculpture *From Memory*, after attempted theft: Graeme and Susan Horsley Collection, Mount Maunganui, 2014

Mei Irihapiti Robin and *Pania of the Reef*, Marine Parade, Napier: Alexander Turnbull Library, Wellington, New Zealand, PAColl-6585-88

Still on Top by James Tissot, c. 1873: Auckland Art Gallery Toi o Tāmaki; gift of Viscount Leverhulme, 1921

Still on Top damaged after theft, August 1998: Auckland Art Gallery Toi o Tāmaki

Fishing Boats Timaru by Archibald Frank Nicoll, 1932: Elizabeth Wearn

Australian Landscape by Robert H. Johnson, c. 1948: Elizabeth Wearn

Scottish Landscape with Sheep by William Menzies Gibb, c. 1910: Elizabeth Wearn

Snowstorm by Rata Lovell-Smith, 1945: Elizabeth Wearn

Still life with irises by Rata Lovell-Smith, 1950: Elizabeth Wearn

CCTV footage of tourist as she steals a fibre work by Alison Naylor: Lakes District Museum and Art Gallery, Arrowtown, March 18, 2013

The bedroom where *Phoenix Rising* by Keith Simpson, 1995, was found in Miharo Street, Rangataua: Constable Lane Demchy, 2014 / New Zealand Police

FURTHER READING

The $12 Million Stuffed Shark: The Curious Economics of Contemporary Art, Don Thompson: Palgrave Macmillan, New York, 2008

Art and Crime: Exploring the Dark Side of the Art World, Noah Charney (ed.): Praeger, Santa Barbara, 2009

Art Crime, John E. Conklin: Praeger, Santa Barbara, 1994

Art Crime and Its Prevention: A handbook for collectors and art professionals, Arthur Tompkins (ed.): Lund Humphries, London, 2016

The Art Detective: Adventures of an Antiques Roadshow Appraiser, Philip Mould: Viking Penguin, New York, 2010

The Art of Forgery: The Minds, Motives and Methods of the Master Forgers, Noah Charney: Phaidon, New York, 2015

Art Theft and the Case of the Stolen Turners, Sandy Nairne: Reaktion Books, London, 2011

Behind the Canvas: An insider's guide to the New Zealand art market, Warwick Henderson: New Holland, Auckland, 2012

Beneath the Surface: McCahon's materials and techniques 1954–66, Sarah Hillary and Kendrah Morgan: Auckland Art Gallery, 2000

Caveat Emptor: The Secret Life of an American Art Forger, Ken Perenyi: W.W. Norton, New York, 2012

A Closer Look: Deceptions and Discoveries, Marjorie E. Wieseman: The National Gallery, London, 2007

Crimes of the Art World, Thomas D. Bazley: Praeger, Santa Barbara, 2010

The Fake: Forgery and Its Place in Art, Sándor Radnóti: Rowman & Littlefield, 1999

Hot Art: Chasing thieves and detectives through the secret world of stolen art, Joshua Knelman: Tin House Books, New York, 2012

James Tissot, Krystyna Matyjaszkiewicz (ed.), Phaidon Press and Barbican Art Gallery, London, 1984

Lost, Stolen or Shredded: Stories of Missing Works of Art and Literature, Rick Gekoski: Profile Books, London, 2013

Museum of the Missing: A History of Art Theft, Simon Houpt: Sterling, New York, 2006

INDEX